Jumpstarting
Your Career

Jumpstarting Your Career

An Internship Guide for Criminal Justice

Second Edition

DOROTHY L. TAYLOR
University of Miami, Emeritus

PEARSON

Prentice
Hall

Upper Saddle River, NJ 07458

Library of Congress Cataloging-in-Publication Data

Taylor, Dorothy L.
    Jumpstarting your career : an internship guide for criminal justice /
Dorothy L. Taylor.— 2nd ed.
      p. cm.
Includes bibliographical references and index.
  ISBN 0-13-117577-7
  1. Criminal justice, Administration of—Study and teaching
(Internship)—United States. l. Title.

  HV9950.T38 2004
  364.973'071'55—dc22

                        2003024816

Publisher: Stephen Helba
Executive Editor: Frank Mortimer, Jr.
Assistant Editor: Korrine Dorsey
Production Editor: Linda Duarte, Pine Tree Composition
Production Liaison: Barbara Marttine Cappuccio
Director of Manufacturing and Production: Bruce Johnson
Managing Editor: Mary Carnis
Manufacturing Buyer: Cathleen Petersen
Creative Director: Cheryl Asherman
Cover Design Coordinator: Miguel Ortiz
Cover Designer: Ruta Fiorino
Editorial Assistant: Barbara Rosenberg
Marketing Manager: Tim Peyton
Formatting and Interior Design: Pine Tree Composition

Pearson Education LTD.
Pearson Education Singapore, Pte. Ltd
Pearson Education, Canada, Ltd
Pearson Education–Japan
Pearson Education Australia PTY, Limited
Pearson Education North Asia Ltd
Pearson Educaçion de Mexico, S.A. de C.V.
Pearson Education Malaysia, Pte. Ltd

ISBN 0-13-117577-7

*This book is dedicated
to my daughter,
Adrienne Hayes-Jones*

Contents

Foreword

Is it ever a good idea to graduate without taking an internship? If you pose this question to Dr. Dorothy Taylor, associate professor emeritus of criminology and sociology at the University of Miami, the answer is, unequivocally, no. The tenor of this advice resounds throughout the second edition of *Jumpstarting Your Career: An Internship Guide for Criminal Justice.* Unlike the first edition, this is a more concise book. Nine chapters are evenly divided into three parts: (1) the concepts of internships, (2) field placement considerations, and (3) evaluation and future careers. As criminal justice agencies continue to give priority and preference to real-world practical experiences, an internship—prior to graduation—is encouraged throughout this book.

After providing the need and rationale for student internships (i.e., field placements), Part I devotes considerable attention to defining internship, its goals and instructional objectives, and the whole field placement process. As a result, readers emerge with a rich historical context for internships and a clearer understanding of the need for students to transition from theory to practice. The author clearly outlines the process of establishing field placements. In addition, pragmatic issues are explored in the broader context of agency goals and social system affiliations. While primarily concerned with matching students with appropriate placements, this section educates students to the practical and political realities of how criminal justice agencies operate. An equally nice feature concerns the practicality of preparing students for an initial interview at a prospective agency.

While internships are highly anticipated, student experiences tend to differ. Thus, much of Part II outlines ways for students to get the most out of their internship experience. Acknowledging that some internships are not entirely stimulating—some are even boring and repetitive—this book guides students in making appropriate site selections that maximize the potential benefits of placements. The author gives equal consideration to the importance of the intern's role and methods of gathering data as well as the role of supervisors in establishing meaningful evaluative criteria. A major strength of this section is clear definition of each party's expectations as it offers useful suggestions for establishing mutually beneficial arrangements. When everyone understands his or her role and what is expected, a good, all-around experience results for the student. In order to meet the various expectations and responsibilities, the author livens the discussion by exploring the influence of ethics in the whole field placement process.

Part III answers the elusive question: How do you evaluate a student's internship performance? The author answers this question by highlighting the role of a field supervision evaluation, a field site evaluation, and the faculty coordinator's evaluation. The confluence of these three criteria is used to assign course grades. This section concludes with a discussion of criminal justice careers relative to various field placements. Perhaps most important in this context is the discussion of taking advantage of potential networking opportunities presented during an internship program. Once students complete internships, the author encourages them to consider the practical applications. Moreover, at what point should students start preparing to choose a career? Is a vocational route more advantageous than, perhaps, a conventional route? These topics are rarely discussed in other courses, but here, each is discussed in sufficient detail. For instance, the author provides constructive advice on how to prepare a résumé, how to investigate potential job opportunities, and how to distinguish circumstances where students may consider continuing their formal education.

In summary, this latest edition—though slightly condensed from its previous version—is well thought out and highly practical. Today, nearly all agencies prefer students with some type of job-related experiences. Many students spend a considerable amount of time pursuing their degrees and graduate with little (if any) practical experiences. Without question, internships are the wave of the future. This being said, this book has great appeal to all criminal justice educators who want to know how to establish, monitor, and evaluate internship programs. Clearly, there is a need to bridge the gap between criminal justice theory and criminal justice practice. This revised edition is a giant step in that direction.

Lee E. Ross
University of Wisconsin-Parkside
Department of Criminal Justice
June 2003

Preface

This book was written for students in the social sciences (criminal justice, criminology, psychology, sociology, and social work) who are beginning a criminal justice internship in a public or private agency. It will also be a useful reference for faculty and agency supervisors. The book focuses on many issues involved in the total internship experience, especially those related to students' personal and professional development during their internship education. A guide of this sort is important because many of my students have, over the past six years, considered their internship among the most influential experiences of their undergraduate careers. At the same time, they have reported that their regular course work provides only indirect, and generally insufficient, preparation for their initial real-world experiences. This book is designed to make the connection between academic course work and the knowledge, skills, and emotional challenges that are found in the professional world of work.

I have attempted to use the best information available from psychology, social work, and other disciplines that the interns will encounter in their various placements. I conducted extensive literature reviews of the leading journals and textbooks in each discipline and consulted with several faculty and agency supervisors in various colleges and universities and internship placements.

Using my personal experience as an intern and my experience coordinating internship placements for hundreds of students, I designed this book to be used as an introductory text on internships that can also be a helpful resource tool for students in their work at the agencies. I hope this book will help readers have a more effective and rewarding work and learning experience.

Acknowledgments

A number of people have influenced and contributed to the second edition of this book. For their encouragement and assistance, I would like to express my gratitude and appreciation to Coramae Richey Mann and Lee E. Ross.

For substantive contributions in helping to shape this book, I would like to thank the many students who have taken my internship course and the field placement supervisors. I would like to especially thank Alia Alinor, Atty. Brian Barakat, Regina Bernadin, Asst. Principal Judy Cobb, Julie Enis, Adam Hellebrand, Petter Kjollerstrom, Melissa Magyar, Sheila Miller, Jason Meringolo, Jill Osenkarski, Andrey Remy, Brooke Samuelson, and LaVaar Scott for contributing chapter opener photos.

A special thanks is extended to Tyra Tate for her computer skills and Danielle Dyer for her contribution to the Resource Guide. Thanks also to Marta Kazmierczak and Jeanie Piard for their contributions to the Instructor's Manual.

The author would also like to thank the following reviewers Clea Andreadis, Middlesex Community College, Bedford, MA; Gary Bayens, Washburn University, Topeka, KS; Anita Blowers, University of North Carolina, Charlotte, NC; and Susan Smith-Cunnien, University of St. Thomas; St. Paul, MN.

Finally, for his patience and understanding while I spent so many hours on the computer, at the library, and performing other tasks involved in producing the second edition of this book, a huge thanks to my husband, Amos Taylor, III, M.D.

Jumpstarting
Your Career

PART I

The Concept of Internships

Long before there was big business, large government, or free-market enterprise, there were interns. In medieval times they were apprenticed to knights and blacksmiths. During the industrial age, children learned trades and skills at low or no pay from the master craftsmen. Thus, as long as there have been skills to learn, there have been interns of some sort.

Today, it is much the same. Stockbrokers, police officers, members of Congress, television producers, and educators are just a few of the persons who take interns under their wings and pass on practical knowledge of their businesses or professions. In addition, many states are in the process of enacting laws that will require prospective teachers to intern with mentors before they are considered for teaching certificates (Barnett, 1990).

Internships give students a much-needed foot in the door to their careers (Scott, 1992, p. 59). Internships also afford companies the opportunity to give prospective employees a semester- or summer-long tryout before deciding whether to hire them.

Indeed, internships are mutually beneficial to both students and organizations. However, not all internship placements are equally beneficial. How does an internship program ensure that students find the best placements for their future career goals? How does a student avoid being little more than a low- or no-paid gofer? These are essential questions in any overview of internships.

Field education courses at various colleges and universities are referred to by different titles, such as internships, practice, and fieldwork. Throughout this book, however, the terms *internship* and *field education* are used interchangeably.

Part I is devoted to exploring the concept of internships. Chapter 1 discusses why students should consider internships, the history of internships, the method of transferring theory into practice with self-directional learning, personal development in relation to coping skills, and professional development that is pertinent to values and ethics. Three common classifications characterize the field education process:

1. *Overview*, in which the student spends time in all branches of an agency to get an overall picture of the agency's function.
2. *Service delivery*, in which the student, under close supervision, actually deals with the agency's clients.
3. *Research*, in which the student uses the facilities of the agency as a laboratory for inquiry into a topic that the student and faculty supervisor have agreed upon. (Blackwelder and Moorman, 1975–1976, p. 2)

Chapter 2 focuses on realistic goal setting prior to starting a field placement, developing pragmatic educational objectives, and methods for assessing one's progress. Chapter 3 provides information on selecting and matching students with the best internship sites, preparing students for the background screening conducted by most criminal justice agencies, and the liability and insurance issues that arise in some agencies.

The client population served is frequently foremost on the minds of the interns when selecting placements. At that time, consideration should also be given to the various types of internship settings available. For example, although the ages of the clients may be the same, an internship in an alternative school setting (for juvenile delinquents only) differs a great deal from an internship in a residential adolescent treatment facility. Similarly, although several of clients served, and the procedural methods used in correctional unsteadiness may be similar to those of a county jail, there will be significant differences that are distinctive to each type of setting. Consider, however, that aside from the clients served and the procedural methods used, if you only have training in one type of setting, an experience in a completely different setting could also be very informative.

As an intern, you will also see how the organization of the agency influences the behavior of the staff. Chapter 4 discusses general agency concerns such as politics and finance as well as providing pertinent information on agency relationships.

1

Defining Internships

QUESTIONS FOR STUDENTS

Why consider an internship?

What is the benefit of integrating classroom knowledge with practical experience?

What are the scholastic, personal, and professional advantages of an internship?

FIELD EDUCATION CONSIDERATION

Why should students consider internships? Although students may be confident that they want careers in criminology or criminal justice, they may not be sure of the specific area in which they wish to specialize. Internships will help them determine the most desirable areas for their future careers or indeed, decide whether they want to remain in the discipline at all. In addition, learning the management procedures of organizations affords significant insights into and understanding of the administration of various agencies. Furthermore, student interactions with agency supervisors, clients, and the agency staff constitute a comprehensive instructional experience that will prove invaluable and will aid in cultivating alliances that may be beneficial in obtaining employment in the future. In some instances, students may be employed by the agencies after the internships end.

If you are looking forward to a career in the field of criminal justice, the following examples offer a few internship possibilities that could lead to a rewarding career in law enforcement.

Police Recruit

The Jacksonville, Florida, Sheriff's Office sponsors a PAID recruit training class. Tuition and annual salary of $32,149 will be paid to those candidates selected to the class. Requirements include results of a Florida Basic Abilities Test (FBAT), an original college transcript denoting a four-year degree—or an original college transcript denoting a minimum of 60 college credit hours with documentation of four years active military service (DD-214), or four years police employment.

Police Officer

Qualifications include possession of a bachelor's degree from a college or university accredited by the American Council on Education or the Council for Higher Education Accreditation. Applicants must pass a physical abilities test, a psychological screening, and a test for controlled substances prior to employment as well as periodically during employment. Applicants must be 21 years of age; meet the state-required minimum qualifications; be of good moral character; have no felony convictions or misdemeanor convictions involving moral character, perjury, or false statements. Applicants must be citizens of the United States. Annual salary is $33,840 (Jacksonville Sheriff's Office, 2003).

Drug Enforcement Agent

Qualifications include possession of a bachelor's degree with a cumulative GPA of 2.95 or higher. Additional consideration will be given to those individuals with degrees in Criminal Justice or related disciplines and who are fluent in Spanish, Russian, Hebrew, Arabic, and Nigerian. Applicants must be U.S. citizens, between 21 and 36 years of age at the time of appointment. They must possess a valid driver's license and be able to obtain a Top Secret security clearance. They must also be in excellent physical condition, have sharp hearing perception, and uncorrected vision of at least 20/200 (Snellen) and corrected vision of 20/20 in one eye and not worse that 20/40 in the other eye. Hearing aids are unacceptable. Substantive professional/administrative or certain law experience may be qualifying. Military experience, pilot/maritime experience, technical/mechanical skills, or accounting/auditing experience may also be qualifying. Along with drug screening, applicants must successfully complete an oral and an exhaustive background investigation (U.S. Department of Justice, 2003a).

Special Agent, Federal Bureau of Investigation (FBI)

Qualifications include any four-year degree—any degree that develops research and analytical skills—from a college or university accredited by one of the regional or national institutional associations recognized by the U.S. Secretary of Education. For example, a law degree is a desirable asset because Special Agents are charged with the duty of investigating violations of U.S. federal laws.

An accounting degree is also desirable because Special Agents trace financial transactions and review/analyze complex accounting records in criminal investigations. Special Agent Accountants often testify in such cases as expert witnesses. An applicant must be a U.S. citizen (or a citizen of the Northern Mariana Islands) and have reached his or her 23rd but not 37th birthday. Every candidate must possess a valid driver's license and must pass a polygraph examination, a drug test, and a color vision test. Other requirements include uncorrected vision not worse than 20/200 (Snellen) and corrected 20/20 in one eye and not worse than 20/40 in the other eye (FBI, 2003b).

Crime Scene Investigator (CSI)

Some positions require a four-year degree in science while others only require a GED or high school diploma. Some agencies require an applicant to become a sworn police officer before becoming a Crime Scene Investigator. The requirements for formal training as a Crime Scene Investigator vary from college to college and university to university. Many community colleges have criminal justice classes that include crime scene investigations. The minimum requirements for this position vary from state to state. To determine what skills, knowledge, and abilities are required—and what education and experience are needed to qualify for the position of Crime Scene Investigator—the best thing to do is to contact the agencies in the geographical area you wish to work (U.S. Department of Justice).

HISTORY OF FIELD PLACEMENTS

Evidence of internships goes back to the Middle Ages, when apprenticeships were served with master craftsmen. This concept continues with field education in various scholastic areas, such as education, law, medicine, nursing, and social services. Several states require persons to undergo internships before they grant certification to practice in these respective disciplines.

From 1968 to 1980, when federal funds were available for internships in criminology and criminal justice, internships became a central component of higher instruction in the field. This funding enabled the Law Enforcement Assistant Administration (LEAA) to grant compensated internships for eight weeks or more at a salary of $65 per week for full-time students. This policy and the LEAA were discontinued in 1980 (Gordon and McBride, 1990).

Although paid criminal justice internships were no longer available, there were still unpaid internships in the field, and the popularity of internships, in general, grew by leaps and bounds during the "intern-crazy nineteen-eighties" (Scott, 1992, p. 59). During that decade competition increased. The baby boom was peaking, with students graduating from universities in droves and seeking employment. Major companies were eager to assist. Businesses such as Digital and Wang, which invested in in-house television studios and additional perks, also invested extravagantly in internship programs.

The abundance of college students and the extensive growth in business enabled corporations to offers internships, which gave them the opportunity to train, observe, and evaluate students for future employment. Summer internships became attractive ways for students to build their résumés.

In the early 1990s, after a decade of growth, the economy stagnated and business decreased, as did many internship programs. For some corporations, internship programs are no longer cost effective. However, internships are still the most effective model for recruiting college graduates for entry-level positions. Therefore, businesses that decrease or abolish their internship programs are "shortsighted and stand to lose their competitive advantage on campus" (Scott, 1992, p. 60).

In addition, as Brenda Brassard, human resources manager for Fidelity Investments in Boston, noted: "Companies are doing less hiring, so the competition is fiercer for internships" (quoted in Wennes, 1993, p. 31). Internships have become significantly more difficult to obtain because there are more students than available positions. When they need to hire more personnel, businesses are more likely to hire those with the pragmatic experience that internships afford. Students are aware of this attitude. As a Wichita State engineering major, Gary Spexarth, said of his internship experience: "I learned a lot more than I ever will, or have, by going to school. . . . it looks so much better when you graduate" (quoted in Wennes, 1993, p. 32).

FROM THEORY TO PRACTICE

Field education has become a central component of the instructional process, affording students a chance for hands-on experience with criminology and criminal justice practitioners. Furthermore, in internship courses, the didactic instruction received in the classroom is enriched, enhanced, and better understood through practical experience in the application of concepts, theories, and principles. (For the principles of internships, see Box 1.1.)

Much of a student's educational instruction occurs in the classroom and consists of note taking and discussion. Learning is restricted to the course content, the instructor's knowledge, the syllabus, and other students' contributions. In this setting, one may or may not choose to participate.

BOX 1.1 *Principles of Internships*

According to Blackwelder and Moorman, internships are a priceless tool in criminology and criminal justice training in that they give students the opportunity to combine information that they learn in the classroom with practical applications. A well-designed internship is an arrangement between a student, a faculty coordinator, and an agency supervisor. The authors stated that internships are based on seven principles (p. 23):

1. Each service-learning intern [should] have at least one *well-defined activity* that is regarded as worthwhile by the organization or group with whom the intern is affiliated, by the intern, and by the faculty mentor.
2. Each service-learning intern [should] develop *specific learning objectives* that can readily be identified and reviewed periodically throughout the work period. The support committee members of faculty and host organization representatives should also develop specific objectives for their participation.
3. Each intern or group of interns [should] be supported by a college-related faculty person and/or community or public organization person. The roles of these *support people* are to assist with task definition, learning objective definition, carrying out of the task, counseling with the intern, and carrying through with the ideas and projects initiated.
4. Each intern [should] *contract* as an independent agent with the organization involved to do the work and pursue the learning objectives in cooperation with a postsecondary educational institution.
5. Each intern [should] have adequate time for private reflection for *assessment* of the worth of his [or her] own experience in providing service to others and learning in a nonschool setting.
6. Each intern [should] produce a report or communication vehicle that is primarily for the agency with which he [or she] is affiliated.
7. Such a *product* should also be illustrative of the learning realized through the experience.

Where possible, regular workshops or meetings [should] be required and arranged to make possible *student-to-student* feedback and accountability. [A learning team of ten to fifteen students meeting regularly (weekly) with supportive mentors is a proven and workable model for encouraging peer-group learning and support.]

Hal Blackwelder and Elliott Moorman, *Internships in Criminal Justice: A Guide to Service-Learning Internships in Agencies of North Carolina's Criminal Justice System.* Raleigh, NC: North Carolina Department of Administration, 1975–1976.
        This booklet is an outgrowth of the Criminal Justice Recruitment and Service-Learning Project, sponsored by the North Carolina Department of Administration during the 1975–1976 academic year. The project was funded by the Governor's Commission on Law and Order with federal funds from LEAA. It was charged with creating new internships (using the model developed by the North Carolina Internship Office) in state and local criminal justice agencies and with cataloging and coordinating existing internship programs in the criminal justice system.

During an internship, the education process is guided by the student (Gordon and McBride, 1990:05). The instructional procedure is guided by actual situations (Dudley, 1980). In addition, examinations and rebuttal are eliminated from the evaluation process.

Although students can apply their knowledge directly and observe particular theories in practice, there may be some they may never observe. It is rewarding to hear from students: "I think internships should be required. The textbooks just don't tell the whole story. Those theories just don't prove out in the real world." For most students, the internships are the first time they are given the chance to test various theories of criminology in a professional setting. In addition, most internship courses require a term paper and several agencies request written narratives. Students' verbal and written communication skills usually improve, as do their listening and interviewing skills.

PERSONAL AND PROFESSIONAL DEVELOPMENT

During the course of their internships, students may be compelled to define, evaluate, or reevaluate their values. By becoming self-aware and learning about their own perspectives and capabilities, they will be able to cultivate the reliance and self-confidence that are crucial to problem solving. This process will be facilitated by their exposure to people who think, believe, and behave differently. These encounters, which are prevalent in many criminal justice agencies, may cause students to examine their own biases and opinions about social issues and become defensive because of their need to reject clients' different values and actions taken by criminal justice agencies. In any event, this exposure will stimulate passions and feelings associated with genuine life circumstances that cannot be generated in the classroom. Some understanding of causal elements in relation to people with problems should empower students to strengthen their convictions about the dignity and value of the persons they are learning to deal with. Assistance from faculty supervisors and agency supervisors should enable them to become more self-aware and thereby to move from subjectivity to objectivity when working with clients.

As interns, students will need to dress properly, maintain an acceptable image, and be dependable. The interns should be prompt, dependable, and efficient. They should also be aware of the significance of performing within an agency context and the necessity of communicating to people in all positions.

In addition to acquiring experience, internships enable students to determine if they really want to work in the field. Most students who approach me for internships are usually considering law school or work in criminal justice agencies (local and federal) or police departments or with delinquent youths. For the twelve years that I have been an internship coordinator, most students complete their training with increased enthusiasm for their career goals. However, a few have found their selected areas unsuitable. For example, a student who was interested in working with delinquent youths reevaluated her goals after she completed her internship at an "alternative school" for juvenile delinquents. As she put it: "These kids are scary. I was afraid every day I was there. The only reason I stayed was because I was always with my supervisor [but] still got kicked one day. These kids are on drugs, they're sexually active, and have no respect for anyone. I've never been around adolescents like these. I had no idea how severe the problem is. I could never do this as a career."

Some of my students' internships have resulted in offers of employment with the organizations. The experience gained and knowledge about how to obtain jobs are invaluable, as are the references and contacts that students acquire.

In most cases, internship experiences are positive. However, in a few situations, the experiences are unsuccessful and the agencies refuse to provide references for pre-employment background investigations because of the interns' unethical conduct or personal and/or professional difficulties during fieldwork.

SUMMARY

Internship programs are the most effective model for recruiting college students for entry-level positions. Although financial subsidies are not automatic, college credits are earned, experience is gained, and invaluable contacts are made for future employment.

The objectives of internships are to help students:

1. Achieve firsthand knowledge and a better perception of criminal justice agencies, their management operations, and the neighborhood forces that influence their structure and procedures.

2. Acquire an awareness of the consequences of social abnormalities upon the public.
3. Combine and implement theories and other information gained in related courses with the practical experience afforded by the field placement.
4. Learn methods and skills that are used in criminal justice agencies, such as observation; organization; and effective communication, listening, and interviewing skills.
5. Develop self-awareness of their values and attitudes toward citizens, the criminal justice system, and the community at large.

Generally, internship programs are designed to assist the students to change their attitudes "from the subjective to the objective through the integration of theoretical class-room material with practical learning experiences" (Keyman, 1997, p. 10).

Because of variations in both students and agencies, not all interns will accomplish all these objectives. However, students may use these criteria to evaluate their pursuit of careers in criminology or criminal justice.

DISCUSSION QUESTIONS

1. How do internships prepare students for field experience and subsequently entry-level jobs?
2. What is the respected conduct and appearance of an intern?
3. During the internship, what are the guiding factors of the education process and the instructional procedure?
4. Upon completion of the internship, how can the individual use what he or she has learned in order to succeed in a respective career?

CHAPTER

2

Goals and Instructional Objectives

QUESTIONS FOR STUDENTS

What field are your career goals related to?

Will the work experience in the agency help you achieve these goals?

After the internship, will you have sufficient credentials to qualify for an agency position?

TYPES OF GOALS

The accumulation of information, appraisal of accomplishments, individual development, and professional growth are four distinctive domains in which students should consider goals and instructional objectives.

The goal of *accumulating information* assists students in acquiring knowledge in areas they knew little about before their internships. It can be achieved, with the aid of the faculty supervisor and agency supervisor, by reading various publications and obtaining organizational information related to the field placement (see Box 2.1).

The goal of *appraising accomplishments* helps students estimate how adequately they have comprehended and performed the assignments of the field

---

BOX 2.1   *One Student's Goals for Accumulating Information*

According to Marta Kazmierczak, her goals for accumulation of information were as follows (p. 3):

1. I would like to better understand the clients and their individual upbringings as they played a part in shaping their criminal minds.
2. I want to attain a better comprehension of the juvenile criminal justice system. I would like to become familiar with the trial process, the incarceration procedures, and rehabilitation.
3. I would like to familiarize myself with the different career opportunities in the criminal justice field, particularly law.

Marta Kazmierczak, "Spring Internship: Miami Halfway House," unpublished manuscript, 2003.

---

placement and the expertise they have acquired in certain skills. It is also necessary for the students to evaluate the conditions in their agencies, distinguish motives for alliances, and examine patterns. For instance, an intern working in the Florida Department of Corrections and Probation and assigned to "the above-standards hallway" (where officers are well organized and perform their jobs well) might establish a goal of developing rapport with these officers to learn more about the job cliques, the division of labor among various officers, and the methods they use to manage their clients better than do the officers in the "regular hallways" (Cecil, 1996).

The goal of *individual development* is attained from the opportunity to mature and develop during the internship process. In this regard, it is important for students to catalog their individual assets to discover their strengths and weaknesses. Assistance from "significant others" may help them clarify their individual-development goals.

The following are illustrations of individual development goals: (1) to learn to work with people from diverse backgrounds, (2) to become aware of how your values and ethics have been shaped by your background and how other people are influenced by theirs, (3) to improve your writing and language skills to increase self-confidence when interacting with supervisors, and (4) to become more assertive in relationship building with co-workers and peers.

The goal of *professional growth* is accomplished by selecting an internship placement relative to a possible career. These aspirations may be distinctive or vague. For example, a student may want a career as a secret service agent or with an organization that provides direct assistance to consumers. Many students whom I have advised have set the goal of acquiring experience as a law clerk in the office of the state attorney to confirm whether they want to attend law school and, if so, what area they wish to specialize in.

PRAGMATIC GOAL SETTING

Beginning interns should have gained basic information about criminology and other associated fields in the classroom and thus should have a solid theoretical foundation for understanding individuals, criminology, criminal justice, and society. It is likely that students chose internships in criminology or criminal justice because they are considering careers in some facet of the discipline, such as law enforcement, corrections, or juvenile justice. During and after their internships, the students will probably ponder many questions related to their career goals, such as these: Was the work satisfactory? Were the agency environment and employee relationships enjoyable? Do I have adequate credentials to qualify for an open position at the agency? If so, do I consider the position a stepping-stone to other positions or a final position?

The students' choice of field placements will depend on their educational, practical, and specific goals. The apparent educational goals are:

- To grasp the procedures of the criminal justice profession
- To apply theories presented in the classroom to actual practice in the field
- To achieve training and gain contacts that will assist in successful transitions to employment in the professional world

The need to distinguish specific goals and to develop techniques for accomplishing them are essential if students are to realize what they have achieved during the field experience. For students to set practical and specific goals, they must first address personal-assessment questions, their skills, and geographic considerations. Furthermore, since most internships do not provide stipends, students need to consider whether they have sufficient funds from college loans and other sources to support themselves and, if applicable, their families during the internship period. Other issues are whether they prefer casework or group work and whether they need constant stimulation or a more stable environment in which things remain pretty much the same from day to day. In establishing realistic goals, students should consider the following:

- The number of hours required at the internship agency
- The responsibilities that the agency will assign to them
- Their personal strengths and weaknesses

- Their skills and competence levels
- Their comprehension of the operations of the criminal justice system and their ability to transfer theory into practice

Once students determine the answers to these and other questions, they and the faculty supervisor can begin to match their criteria to those of various agencies and areas in which they are interested.

DEVELOPING EDUCATIONAL OBJECTIVES

After the students have established their goals in the four domains, they determine distinctive educational objectives to specify how they aim to achieve their goals. It is imperative that they confer with the agency supervisor and the faculty coordinator to guarantee that the objectives are practical, obtainable, and appraisable. The objectives serve as guides to ascertaining the students' accountability at the placement site, as well as tools to measure the students' general achievement and as a foundation for dialogue during routine supervisory conferences.

The following are examples of educational objectives that may be established:

1. I will keep a weekly journal of my thoughts, feelings, and experiences from my internship.
2. I will discuss these issues with my agency (field) supervisor, my faculty supervisor, and the people I am assigned to work with.
3. I will get feedback from my agency supervisor regarding the impression the staff have of me to compare with how I think I am perceived by the staff.

An intern working in a probation department established the following educational objectives to achieve her goal of professional development:

1. I will learn about violation reports and drug tests from the officer assigned to these functions.
2. I will compare reports and confer with the officer regarding improvement.
3. I will continue to learn about violation reports and drug testing for the duration of my field experience.

Permaul (1981) noted that educational objectives for the goal of accumulating information should consist of the following:

1. Become aware of and informed about the topic.
2. Analyze, synthesize, and generalize the readings and discussions.
3. Take action or think about how you might act in specific situations.

An intern working in a center for girls in Dade County, Florida, wanted to understand more about sexual abuse, which many of the girls had encountered. She set the following objectives for achieving the goal of accumulating information:

1. I will review the sociological and criminological literature regarding the topic.
2. I will plan sessions with the staff social worker to gain a better understanding of the girls and sexual abuse.
3. I will confer with my agency supervisor to gain approval for conducting in-depth interviews with the sexually abused girls.

PROGRESS ASSESSMENT

Since the internship processes allow the students to become self-conducted learners, assessments of their progress in achieving their educational objectives and goals are their primary obligation. These tasks will assist the students to realize whether their goals and objectives are practical and obtainable in their field-placement settings.

Our students have found written assessments, audio- or videotaping, and feed-back to be helpful techniques:

1. *Written assessments* to your faculty supervisor in the form of notes, a journal, or e-mail will compel you to consider your experiences carefully and will provide you with a historical perspective as you progress through your internship.
2. *Audio- or videotaping* is also useful in evaluating your skills. Recording interviews with clients, victims, witnesses, and others can help you assess your competency, especially with assistance and feedback from your agency supervisor. You should explain to the person you are interviewing that you are recording the sessions and obtain written consent.
3. *Feedback* from supervisors and peers is another effective technique for evaluating your skills and competency levels. Feedback received from discussing your progress in regular meetings with your faculty and agency supervisors and in seminars with your peers may cause you to reevaluate your goals and develop new goals and objectives.

SUMMARY

Education is a continuous process that should be perceived as transpiring through formal and informal procedures. The internship program illustrates the many techniques by which students can take part in the educational process. This chapter has focused on four major goals that several internship programs have considered necessary for forming field education experiences: accumulating information, appraising accomplishments, individual development, and personal growth. Once their goals are clarified, students must determine precise educational objectives that allow them to attain their goals and evaluate their progress.

Flexibility is key to a successful internship experience. A student should be ready to adjust his or her goals, if necessary, as the field-placement environment becomes familiar. The issues addressed in this chapter are important for students' personal and professional development during their internships. They will also be helpful in furthering professional development in future jobs, whether in criminal justice or social service agencies.

DISCUSSION QUESTIONS

1. What tasks will assist students with realizing whether their goals and objectives are practical and obtainable in their field of study?
2. What are four distinctive domains in which students should consider goals and instructional objectives?
3. Consider a field you would like to pursue in the future. Create three educational objectives to serve as a guide to ascertain accountability at the placement site and to reassure your general achievement.
4. What is the key to a successful internship experience?

CHAPTER

3

Field-Placement Process

QUESTIONS FOR STUDENTS

What are your long-term professional aspirations?

What courses have you taken that may be relevant to an internship?

Is your daily schedule conducive to the hours required by an internship?

SELECTING THE INTERNSHIP SITE

The first step in selecting the internship site is to consider which agency will provide the best experience relevant to your career goals. If you want to work in law enforcement, you should consider a placement in a local, state, or federal law enforcement agency. If juvenile delinquency is of interest to you, the juvenile justice system affords a myriad of placements, such as the juvenile court, alternative schools, and residential treatment facilities. Many internship programs provide placements within local areas near colleges or universities. However, in some instances, schools place students in out-of-state agencies.

If your college program provides statewide, regional, or out-of-state internships, you should consider and discuss these possibilities with your internship coordinator a semester or two before you intend to begin the internship. You will need to know about the placement procedure, academic prerequisites, and application deadlines. (For sample information on academic prerequisities, see Box 3.1.) You should keep in mind that most internships are not paid, although some agencies provide a small stipend if permitted by the school.

In some schools the placements are the sole responsibility of the students, while in other schools individual departments control all components of the internship process. As I have done in the Sociology Department of the University of Miami, many internship coordinators have identified internship supervisors and sites that are used annually and require students to consider these placements first. However, if students find contacts for placements that are either more relevant to their career goals or closer to their homes, the coordinator may consider these placements after they visit and approve the sites and appoint staff supervisors. The final decision for the internship placement should belong to the student.

PROPER STUDENT PLACEMENT

Once the site has been selected, the process of matching the student with a site plays an important role in guaranteeing a positive experience for both student and agency. I schedule half-hour appointments for each perspective intern to discuss

---

BOX 3.1   *Requirements*

In order to intern:

1. You must have completed Soc 101 and Soc 271.
2. You must have an overall GPA of 2.5 or higher.
3. You must decide what area of the field or which specific agency you would like to intern with.
4. You must turn in all required forms to the Internship Coordinator by the deadline specified.
5. You must register for Soc 365 (Internships) and pay for 6 semester hours of credit by the university's deadline date for fee payment.
6. You are required to complete 240 hours at your internship placement.
7. You are further required to complete a satisfactory term paper, on your agency, which will be due during final exam week.

For additional information, please contact the Internship Coordinator at (305) 284–6038.

matching. Some students are not sure of their career goals at the time, and after some discussion, I advise them to schedule another appointment when they have thought through the options more clearly. Students should approach this process attentively, so that their initial internship experience is positive. Since a student will be spending a good deal of time (from two to four days a week) and resources on this endeavor, each has the right to get the most benefit from it.

Over the years, I obtained information pertinent to efficient and successful matching from students during our interviews. On the basis of Baird's (1996) model, I then generated an information form for collecting data on students' characteristics for matching interns with placement sites. Matching these data with information from various agencies increases the probability that the placements will be successful.

THE FIELD-PLACEMENT INTERVIEW

You have been notified that your paperwork has been received and processed by the agency and that you have been accepted for an interview. The interview is the second important step in the placement process because it gives you the opportunity to have a one-to-one discussion with the agency supervisor and occasionally with other significant personnel who will be involved in the selection process. This is the time to address issues, concerns, and questions regarding the agency's responsibilities and yours as an intern. The interview is a crucial point because if the outcome is not satisfactory for either party, one or both can decide that the placement seems unsuitable. In some cases, either the student or the agency does not determine that the placement is unsuitable until a week or so into the internship. In such a case, some schools may be willing to reassign the student to another agency, only under extraordinary circumstances, but the agency has to be one that does not require an extensive background check and could accommodate the student in making up any lost hours to fulfill the internship credits.

To make a good impression at your interview, you should thoroughly research the organization's history, missions, and functions. You may obtain such information on the Internet, from the library, by visiting the agency, and by discussions with your internship coordinator and/or other students who have interned at the agency; in some colleges, coordinators may have brochures on several agencies. In addition, you should dress properly, by which I mean that a young man should wear a dress shirt, a tie, a suit or sports jacket, and dress shoes, and a young woman should wear a dress or suit (in warm climates, you may dispense with a jacket). When in doubt, check with your internship coordinator.

It should be noted that the proper dress for interviewing may not be the proper dress for work once you receive the internship. This is one of the issues that should be addressed during the interview. In some juvenile residential facilities, the preferred dress is jeans, T-shirts, and sneakers, while in other juvenile programs (such as Guardian Ad Litem in Miami), a dress or suit is required because of the short notice given for court appearances.

To avoid a negative image during the interview, *do not* chew gum, smoke, or wear strong perfume or after-five clothing. *Do not* be late; arrive at least 5 to 10 minutes early for your appointment. If you feel the need to take along a friend or someone has to drive you, leave the person in the reception area and go into the interview alone.

The potential supervisor will have a number of questions for you. You should also be prepared with questions regarding the internship. Some authors (Hersh and Poey, 1987; Pitts, 1992) have offered useful suggestions for prospective interns in preparing for interviews. For example, they have suggested that you:

- Describe to the interviewer why you want to work in this particular agency and what your goals there will be.
- Inquire about your expected duties, duties performed by former interns, and the hours and shift you would be assigned.
- Ask your interviewer about his or her experience as a professional and training and experience as a supervisor.

Some students have expressed anxiety regarding the interviewing process. Role-playing the interview with your coordinator or others or speaking with a student who previously interviewed at the agency will help to ease some of the anxiety.

Informal Background Check

In most internship programs, the internship coordinator conducts an initial screening to determine a student's eligibility for an internship. Then, depending on the type of agency and its policy, the agency providing the internship often does a second background check. All criminal justice agencies require background checks. The program's screening focuses on the student's academic standing, background information (previous course work) related to the placement, and individual responsibility, as well as evaluations by the faculty. The agency's screening is usually much more extensive. For example, one of my students who was applying for an internship with the U.S. Secret Service told me that his brother was in the armed forces and stationed in Germany (information that he included in his Secret Service application), so during the agency's background check the student's brother and wife were investigated.

After you have submitted your application, résumé, and cover letter and have been interviewed, there is still a possibility that you may have to submit additional information about your background or give authorization for a background check. This is another reason why it is important to be truthful on the initial application that you submit to your internship coordinator. Affirmative action and antidiscrimination laws can prevent most agencies in the public and private sectors from asking questions that are not job related. Law enforcement and other criminal justice agencies, however, have more leeway in their background investigations, and some agencies use polygraph tests to check on personal practices and criminal history, honesty, and reliability. Drug and alcohol use may also be checked, and some agencies may ask you to submit to drug testing.

The background check is a serious matter. If you are truly interested in a career in the field of criminal justice or the discipline of criminology, you must constantly avoid unethical or criminal conduct (see Chapter 7 for a discussion of Ethics).

THE AGENCY SCREENING PROCESS

Just as you are considering whether an agency is an appropriate placement for you, an agency's administrators also have to decide if you are eligible to be an intern for the agency. In making this decision, the administrators will review your application, cover letter, résumé, and transcript; interview you; and check your background. Therefore, you should be prepared for all these aspects of the selection process.

Completing an Application, Résumé, and Cover Letter

If the application is a standard form, you should type or print it and complete it as thoroughly as possible. You should then submit it to your internship coordinator six to eight weeks prior to the beginning of the proposed internship or in whatever time frame the coordinator deems necessary. (For a sample application, see Figure 3.1.)

The school's application usually asks for the following information: the semester and year of the requested internship, personal demographics, grade-point average, whether you have a driver's license and have an automobile at your disposal, whether you have taken courses that are prerequisites for an internship, desired agency, and record of violations. It is important that you sign the application in good faith because a false statement can be grounds for termination.

The résumé and cover letter should also be submitted to your internship coordinator within the specified period. This material, along with other pertinent information, will be forwarded to the agency that is considering your placement. After the agency has reviewed your file and considered you an acceptable candidate, you will probably have to complete another application for the agency. The internship coordinator may provide a standard résumé as a guide. (See Figure 3.2 for a sample résumé form.)

On this form you provide personal data, educational data, information on awards and hobbies, employment history, and references. Even though this form of

SEMESTER/YEAR YOU WOULD   DATE OF APPLICATION
LIKE TO INTERN _____   _____
NAME _____   SS# _____
LOCAL
ADDRESS _____   PHONE _____
PERMANENT
ADDRESS _____   PHONE _____

YEAR IN SCHOOL _____   DOB _____ OVERALL G.P.A. _____
DO YOU HAVE A CAR? _____ GRADUATION DATE _____
HAVE YOU COMPLETED: YES   NO   TAKING NOW   GRADE
SOC 101 (INTRO TO SOCIOLOGY)   ____   ____   _____   _____
SOC 271 (INTRO TO CRIM JUSTICE)   ____   ____   _____   _____

WHERE DO YOU WISH TO INTERN? _____
NAME OF PERSON IN CHARGE OF INTERNS AT THE
AGENCY _____
ADDRESS OF AGENCY _____
_____ PHONE _____
MANY AGENCIES MAY NOT ACCEPT STUDENTS WITH CONVICTIONS. IN ORDER TO FACILI-
TATE PLACEMENT, PLEASE ANSWER THE FOLLOWING:

HAVE YOU EVER BEEN CONVICTED OF A FELONY OR A FIRST-DEGREE MISDEMEANOR?
YES _____ NO _____
IF YES, PLEASE SPEAK WITH THE COORDINATOR PRIOR TO PLACEMENT.

LIST MOVING VIOLATIONS (i.e., speeding, careless driving, etc.)
_____
_____

6 CREDIT HOURS (MINIMUM 240 HOURS AT AGENCY AND TERM PAPER).

YOU MUST SIGN THIS APPLICATION. A FALSE STATEMENT ON ANY PART OF THIS APPLICA-
TION MAY BE GROUNDS FOR NOT RECEIVING AN INTERNSHIP PLACEMENT, OR FOR BEING
TERMINATED FROM AN AGENCY AFTER PLACEMENT. ALL OF MY STATEMENTS ARE MADE IN
GOOD FAITH, AND ARE TRUE AND COMPLETE.

_____   _____
STUDENT SIGNATURE   DATE

Figure 3.1   Sample Internship Application

résumé is acceptable, I recommend that you compose and type an individual résumé. It makes a better impression and will give you experience that you will need later in competing in the job market. (See Figure 3.3 for a sample typed résumé.)

Regardless of which type you select, the résumé should be typed, properly spaced, and contain no typographical errors. This internship résumé should be modified when you apply for paid positions. Ideally, the résumé should be one page and should not exceed two pages.

When you apply for an internship (or other position), the cover letter should indicate why you have chosen the agency; what special knowledge, skills, or train-

```
┌─────────────────────────────────────────────────────────────────────────────┐
│ NAME _____ SS# _____        │
│ LOCAL ADDRESS _____         │
│ _____         │
│ TELEPHONE _____ MARITAL STATUS _____          │
│ DATE OF BIRTH _____ YEAR IN SCHOOL _____          │
│ EDUCATION                                                                      │
│ HIGH SCHOOL _____          │
│ DATE GRADUATED _____           │
│ COLLEGE _____           │
│ MAJOR _____ MINOR _____ GPA _____       │
│ SOCIOLOGY COURSES COMPLETED (COURSE NUMBER AND TITLE):                          │
│ _____  _____             │
│ _____  _____             │
│ _____  _____             │
│ SCHOLASTIC AWARDS, STUDENT ORGANIZATIONS, HOBBIES, INTERESTS                    │
│ _____          │
│ _____          │
│ WORK EXPERIENCE (EMPLOYER'S NAME, ADDRESS, AND TELEPHONE)                       │
│ ____/____ TO ____/____  _____           │
│                          _____          │
│                          POSITION _____            │
│ ____/____ TO ____/____  _____           │
│                          _____          │
│                          POSITION _____            │
│ ____/____ TO ____/____ ____                                                     │
│                          _____          │
│                          POSITION _____            │
│ REFERENCES:                                                                     │
│ 1. Name/Title _____ PHONE #(____) _____             │
│    Address: _____             │
│ 2. Name/Title _____ PHONE #(____) _____             │
│    Address: _____             │
│ 3. Name/Title _____ PHONE #(____) _____             │
│    Address: _____             │
└─────────────────────────────────────────────────────────────────────────────┘
```

Figure 3.2   Sample Student Internship Résumé

ing you will bring to the agency; and what you expect to learn at the agency. *Do not treat the cover letter lightly;* it is an important consideration for the agency in arriving at a placement decision. (See Figure 3.4 for a sample cover letter.)

Your internship coordinator may send a standard cover letter with your documents. However, if the cover letter is your responsibility, remember that it is your introduction to the agency. Therefore, address the letter to a specific person (whose name you may obtain from the coordinator), be brief, and make sure that all words are spelled correctly.

Michelle A. Lee

Current Address:
6091 NW 15th Avenue, Apt. 3
Miami, FL 33124-8156
(305) 243-4593
MLEE@STUDENTS.MIAMI.EDU

Permanent Address:
2121 Windy Hill Road
Marietta, GA 30314
(770) 435-3315

OBJECTIVE   To obtain a position that utilizes my secretarial skills, builds upon my criminology skills, and provides opportunity for growth in the law enforcement field.

EDUCATION

UNIVERSITY OF MIAMI Coral Gables, FL.
Bachelor of Science, May 2003, Majors: Psychology/Criminology
Minor: Business Administration
Major GPA: 3.37/3.42

RELEVANT COURSES

PSYCHOLOGY
Abnormal Psychology	Psychology of Women
Emotion	Organization Psychology
Psychology of Drugs and Behavior	

CRIMINOLOGY
Criminology	Criminal Justice
Juvenile Delinquency	Corrections
Law and Society	Theories of Deviant Behavior

BUSINESS ADMINISTRATION
Accounting	Marketing
Fundamentals of Finance	Organizational Behavior

SKILLS

- Microsoft Word
- Power Point
- Excel
- Publisher
- Print Artist
- PageMaker

HONORS AND ACTIVITIES

- Alpha Kappa Alpha Sorority
- Deans List

Figure 3.3   Sample Résumé

WORK EXPERIENCE	FEDERAL BUREAU OF PRISONS Miami, FL
January 03–May 03	Student Intern

- Involved in the daily operation of the prison's Community Correction Office
- Assisted staff in assigning inmates to appropriate community corrections center
- Assist in evaluating community corrections center's performance regarding contract compliance, including prerelease programs personnel and facility

August 02–December 02 **UNIVERSITY OF MIAMI WELLNESS CENTER** Coral Gables, FL
- Student Assistant
- Processed facility reservation requests for special events
- Coordinated, maintained, and distributed all event schedules
- Maintained calendar and arranged departmental meetings

August 01–December 01 **DEPARTMENT OF MINORITY STUDENT AFFAIRS**
- Student Assistant
- Assisted Office Liaison to student body in creation of departmental publications
- Assisted in maintaining current mailing list of all minority students
- Assisted in planning activities and events for students

January 00–December 00 **DEPARTMENT OF STUDENT LIFE**
- Student Assistant
- Assisted Office Assistant in securing reservations for meetings and special events
- Assisted in greeting and assisting all visitors
- Assisted in updating various forms

Figure 3.3   (Cont.)

If your coordinator is handling this internship, he or she will receive the response from the agency, and in some instances you will also. If you are handling the internship and have not received a reply within two to three weeks, it is appropriate to inquire, by telephone or mail, about the status of your application. This contact should be made with the person to whom you addressed the cover letter.

LIABILITY COVERAGE

Since internship courses have become a central part of several social science degree programs, they have heightened universities' and internship agencies' concern about liability issues (Schultz, 1992). Thus, there seems to be a need for mutual understanding between universities and agencies of the legal responsibilities and potential liabilities of each. As Schultz (1992) pointed out, both parties to

6091 NW 15th Avenue, Apt 3
Coral Gables, FL 33124-8156
May 5, 2003

Ms. Andrea Johnson
Community Corrections Manager
Federal Bureau of Prisons
401 North Miami Avenue
Miami, FL 33178

Dear Ms. Johnson:

I am writing to express my interest in the student intern position that is available. I am currently a senior at the University of Miami and will be receiving my degree in both Criminology and Psychology in May 2003.

I am very interested in a career in criminal justice and would enjoy working for the federal government after graduation. This internship will give me an opportunity to learn more about the criminal justice system. I have been working in an office for over three years. I am responsible for data entry, filling, organizing, and other things that will be helpful to your office.

I am very excited about the prospect of interning with your office. I look forward to hearing from you. Thank you for your consideration.

Sincerely,

Michelle A. Lee

Michelle A. Lee

Figure 3.4   Sample Cover Letter

an internship agreement have the right to be informed of the legal implications; knowledge of potential liabilities can alert program directors to methods for minimizing unnecessary risks and managing them effectively. Also, information about liability issues can alleviate the concerns of placement supervisors at agencies, who may be cautious about undertaking such arrangements unless they understand these issues at the outset.

The main concern of the internship coordinator and the university is injury to the student while at the field placement or while involved in internship-related activities. The decision about whether you can participate in various placement activities is the sole responsibility of your field supervisor. You, however, have the right to decline to participate in any event that you think is unsafe. Before you begin an internship, the coordinator may discuss safety guidelines that are pertinent to your placement. For instance, all U.S. police departments and schools have agreements that students who participate in "ride-alongs" are not permitted outside the patrol cars or to be in areas where officers respond to violent encounters. In addition, students who intern for the bureau of prisons are not allowed to enter the cell blocks or recreational facilities unescorted, and those who intern at the juvenile court are not allowed to conduct home visits unaccompanied.

You will probably be required by your internship coordinator and your field placement supervisor to sign a consent form that you have been informed of the inherent dangers of the internship and are releasing the school and/or the agency from liability. (See Figure 3.5 for a sample student agreement, including a release-of-liability clause.) These forms serve to signify a mutual understanding of the

---

This statement is to affirm my understanding of the conditions under which I am applying for a Criminal Justice Internship in the Department of Sociology at the University of Miami.

I understand that in order to intern I must:

1. Have a completed SOC 101 and SOC 271;
2. Have at least an overall G.P.A. of 2.5;
3. Complete 240 hours at the internship placement;
4. Agree to complete the term paper assigned by the Internship Coordinator and made a part of my permanent file.

I understand that during my internship I will not be identified as anything other than a student intern, and I agree not to place myself or allow myself to be placed in dangerous situations nor allow myself to be used in any undercover capacity. Further, I agree to release the University of Miami and the Department of Sociology and the officers and faculty of same from all legal liability for any injury that I may sustain during the performance of activities as a student intern.

I understand that in order to fulfill the academic requirements of the internship program, I must:

(1) Complete a participant-observation type term paper and a satisfactory evaluation(s) in a timely manner;
(2) Receive satisfactory evaluation(s) from my intern supervisor.

I further understand that my failure to fulfill these requirements will result in an unsatisfactory grade for the internship course.

I hereby accept these conditions under which my application for a criminal justice internship is being made.

Signed: _____

Date: _____

Figure 3.5 Sample Student Agreement

risks involved in interning. Black (1987) and Schultz (1992), however, warned that these forms are not completely binding against future legal actions or recovery.

Schultz (1992) suggested that it is necessary for students to receive insurance protection, but that obtaining such insurance can be complicated because of unique problems associated with health care, workers' compensation, and personal liability. Here I should point out that during my twelve years as an internship coordinator, no student, agency, or my school has been sued for an alleged act of misfeasance or malfeasance.

Since health care insurance is not provided for interns at most placement sites, you should make sure that your university's student health plan provides appropriate coverage. If you are a part-time student, you should discuss the issue with an appropriate school advocate.

Regarding workers' compensation, as a general rule, if you are receiving a stipend for services rendered to the agency, you would be covered. However, because the laws vary from state to state, it would be wise to seek expert opinion within your local area.

SUMMARY

Before deciding on your internship placement, you should have some idea of your long-term goals, even if they change in the future. It is always helpful if you have taken courses relevant to your desired internship. Another consideration is whether your schedule will allow you time to participate in an internship.

Many students are not sure of their career goals when choosing their placements. If you are not certain of your goals, schedule an appointment with the internship coordinator in your department and receive guidance.

The locations of internships vary from school to school. Some coordinators provide placements within local areas while others provide regional and out-of-state internships.

Although many coordinators have a list of participating agencies, they also are open to students' suggesting and arranging new internship placements and supervisory contacts.

Criminal justice agencies perform in-depth background investigations, including family members and friends.

The three most important forms required by internship coordinators are the résumé, the cover letter, and the background application. A sample of each is included in this chapter.

During the agency interview, you will make a good impression by having some basic knowledge of the organization and perhaps of the agency supervisor. It is appropriate for you to inquire about the amount of time the supervisor will have to work directly with you. The proper attire for this occasion is a tie and a jacket for young men and a dress or suit for young women. Depending on the agency, the proper interviewing attire may not be the proper work attire. This issue should be addressed during the interview.

The intensity of the background screening depends on the agency's policy. The Secret Service screens more thoroughly than the probation department because these agencies have different levels of responsibility. The background check is a serious matter. To secure a career in the criminal justice field, your behavior must be above reproach, and you must avoid unethical or criminal conduct.

With regard to liability and insurance, the main concern of the internship coordinator and school is injury to the student. Although your field supervisor decides whether you can participate in placement activities, it is your right to decline to engage in any activity that you deem unsafe.

You will be asked by your internship coordinator and agency supervisor to sign a "hold harmless" consent form that you have been informed of the inherent dangers of the internship and are releasing the school and/or agency for any liability. Health care insurance is not provided for interns at most placement sites. Generally, worker's compensation is considered only if you are a full-time intern and are receiving a stipend and are injured on the job. Because laws regarding workers' compensation vary from state to state, you should seek expert opinion regarding this issue.

DISCUSSION QUESTIONS

1. How should a student go about selecting an internship site? What factors should be considered in this decision?

2. During a field-placement interview, how should the student present him- or herself in order to make a lasting impression?

3. In preparation for the agency screening process, how important is the professionalism of a student? How should a student prepare his or her application, resume, and cover letter?

4. Understanding and abiding by the liability coverage of a field-placement agency is extremely important. How should the agency, the educational facility, and the student come to an agreement regarding safety issues during an internship?

CHAPTER

4

Pragmatic Agency Concerns, Agency Goals, and Social System Affiliations

---

QUESTIONS FOR STUDENTS

What impact does bureaucracy have on your agency's performance?

How does bureaucracy affect the financial disbursements of your agency?

In what way does judicial consideration influence the efficiency of your agency's employees?

BUREAUCRACY AND CONTROL

This chapter provides insight into three systems—bureaucratic, financial, and judicial—that influence the criminal justice system and consequently, your agency. *Control* is a key word in the administration of justice. For instance, the ability to control people, evident in the way that laws are enacted and enforced, results in a pervasive bureaucratic (political) influence throughout the criminal justice system, from the police to the courts to the prisons. Those who study "critical" criminology report that the criminal justice system mirrors the values of individuals and groups with political power. This type of control may be more evident for those who intern in small communities where one family or group has control over the limited political and economic existence of the citizenry. In larger communities, however,

30

criminal justice special-interest groups compete for the power necessary to sway their communities' judgment.

Most of you will intern for agencies in large communities where special-interest groups are constantly attempting to accomplish their goals through this bureaucratic process. According to Cox and Wade (1998), despite the negative connotations of bureaucratic corruption or any other type of exploitation of the criminal justice system for individual profit, the relationship between politics and criminal justice should not be considered negative, but "necessary and desirable in a democratic society" (p. 24). Some researchers claim that special-interest groups are beneficial in helping criminal justice practitioners become more aware and observant of the social values of the community (Bent, 1974). During your internship, you will be introduced to other important terms related to bureaucratic, financial, and judicial considerations, such as *politics, power, authority,* and *discretion.*

Politics

Lasswell (1958, p. 5) stated it very simply: "Politics is who gets what, when, and how." As an intern, you will observe criminal justice practitioners developing mutual alliances shaped by political considerations. One example is the relationship between political parties and the appointments of prosecutors, police chiefs, and judges, among others. Another example is the organization of special-interest groups by criminal justice practitioners, such as law enforcement coalitions and criminal justice task forces on corrections, which seek to influence policymaking decisions that will benefit agencies' goals. In 1986 the American Correctional Association (ACA), an organization of correctional workers, was awarded a grant by the National Institute of Corrections, U.S. Department of Justice, to develop a handbook on public correctional policies. The twenty-one public correctional policies were endorsed by the ACA.

During your internship, you will note that although there is an overall political influence, it may not be felt on a daily basis. In Wilson's (1968) study on the association between politics and the police, little day-to-day political influence on community policing was reported. However, the community's bureaucratic culture was significant in determining the selection of the police chief, the manner of law enforcement, and the character of departmental policy. No matter the style of bureaucracy, police departments depend on politicians for resources, such as personnel, salaries, and benefits, that are negotiated through official representatives of local residents. Chambliss (1994) observed that through their votes police officers, as community residents, can influence the results of elections and hence play a part in selecting politicians for these negotiations.

Those of you who are interning in prosecutors' offices may observe the political relationship between the police and prosecutors. Remember that prosecutors are politicians, whose election is usually supported by primary political groups, which gives them considerable discretionary powers. Police officers also exercise significant discretion in making arrests, and their relationship with prosecutors greatly influences that discretion. For example, original arrest cases are ultimately sent to the prosecutor for additional preparation. Consequently, the practices and wishes of the prosecutor influence the types of arrests the police officers make and the kinds of cases the officers submit to the prosecutor. On the other hand, even though a police officer may believe that an arrest is warranted and the case should go to court, the prosecutor, in fear of losing a difficult case and thereby losing political support, could take advantage of his or her position and discretionary powers and drop the case. Of course, this is not the norm. The need of the public, the police, and the courts to protect their vested interests usually limits the police officers' and prosecutors' use of their discretionary powers.

Politics also plays a considerable role at higher levels of the criminal justice system. The next level for the prosecutor is usually a judgeship, which is rarely attained without the support of a political party. In several states, the citizens elect county and circuit court judges, but in others, such as Florida, judges are appointed by the state governors on recommendations from nonpartisan judicial nominating commissions. Federal judges are appointed by the president with confirmation by the Senate. Baker and Meyer (1980) reported that most appointed federal judges are of the same political party as the president. An appointment to the Supreme Court is also political, as are the Court's decisions to hear cases and who will write the majority opinions (Woodward and Armstrong, 1979). Just as the corrections field has its associations, police officers have their local and national political organizations. Attorneys are represented by local and state bar associations and the American Bar Association. Two additional arms of corrections are state parole boards, whose members are politically appointed, and probation departments, whose probation officers are hired by chief justices of circuit courts or panels of judges.

Power and Authority

On the basis of Blau's (1964) discussion of politics, *power* may be defined as the ability of individuals or organizations to force their convictions repeatedly on others despite resistance, and *authority* may be defined as the appropriate use of power by people in distinctively appointed capacities.

As was shown earlier with regard to politics and power, power and authority are perplexingly intermixed. Politics, power, and authority work together when, for example, the society allows people in particular capacities the privilege of using (or misusing) specific types of power, although the bestowal of this privilege is a political process in which individuals or groups are elected to positions of authority (Cox and Wade, 1998). It is widely believed that political power and authority in the criminal justice system have been used by the wealthy against those without money, power, or authority. Several studies have reported that upper-income groups are less suspicious of the police than are lower-income groups, and that blacks of all income levels distrust the police (Flowers, 1988; Kramer, 1992; Mann, 1993; Taylor et al., 1994). In addition, many writers have reported that black youths receive harsher treatment by the police than do their white counterparts (Taylor and Bing, 1995). Of course, these are issues of discretion, which are discussed below.

During your internship, observe the nature and magnitude of the connection among politics, power, and authority at your agency. This will help you appreciate the overall effect of these elements on the criminal justice system and the practitioners who operate within it, as well as the direct influence on your agency.

Discretion

Although the term *discretion* pervades the criminal justice system, there is no consensus on its meaning. Cole (1970, p. 477) broadly defined it as "the authority to make decisions without reference to specific rules or facts, using instead one's own judgment," whereas Newman (1970, p. 479) defined it as "the authority to choose among alternative actions or of not acting at all." Some social scientists embrace Newman's definition, while others think it is useless. LaFave and Scott (1972) concluded that discretion derives from the lack of a precise and rational body of criminal law and the failure of state legislatures to draft precise criminal codes that specify all behavior considered criminal and omit all other behavior. As they noted, "In part the problem is the result of poor draftsmanship and a failure to revise the criminal law to eliminate obsolete provisions" (pp. 18–19). During your internship, it is important for you to be aware of the many faces of discretion: public, police, prosecutorial, defense, judicial, and correctional.

Interns working in police departments, public defenders' offices, and prosecutors' offices are introduced immediately to *public discretion* and are surprised about the significant magnitude of the discretionary powers of community residents; that is, upon observing a suspicious or criminal act, each citizen has the discretion to report or not to report it. Many studies have indicated that thousands of crimes in this country go unreported because many citizens are reluctant to exercise this discretion (Flowers, 1988; Livingston, 1996; Mann, 1993). During classroom discussions, students have described how citizens' discretion about testifying or not testifying has influenced civil and criminal cases. This same discretion is used with regard to decisions to break or abide by the law and whether to exercise one's vote for or against various law enforcement issues.

"Differential enforcement of the law" (Flowers, 1988) is another phrase used for *police discretion*. Police officers have the power to issue traffic tickets or just to reprimand drivers, to arrest or not to arrest suspects, to investigate or not to investigate crimes, to shoot or not to shoot, and so on. However, as mentioned earlier, an officer's ability to arrest and/or investigate could be jeopardized by a citizen's discretion.

Two types of law enforcement are practiced by the police: full enforcement and selective enforcement. Some police officers believe that full enforcement of the law is "seldom possible or desirable" (Cox and Wade, 1998, p. 37). The power to use personal judgment to decide to arrest a suspect or to investigate a case is essentially selective law enforcement. Because the daily actions of police officers are seldom evaluated administratively or judicially, these discretionary powers can easily turn from discretion to racism, discrimination, violence, and various other types of unlawful enforcement. Prosecutors and judges, however, have the power to reverse the decisions of police officers, except in cases of shootings, which are handled by the Internal Affairs Divisions of police departments, which oversee the behavior of police officers. Nevertheless, these first personal judgments by police officers are considered a basic discretionary power (Flowers, 1988).

Prosecutors (also called district attorneys, state's attorneys, or chief prosecutors) use *prosecutorial discretion* to prosecute or not to prosecute, which many criminal justice practitioners believe is the most powerful of all the discretionary powers. As Neubauer (1992, p. 102), stated: "The prosecutor is the most powerful official in the criminal courts." The prosecutor is considered the principal law enforcement official of the community, with the basic responsibility of protecting the public. This is regarded as the foremost position in the criminal justice system because police officers, defense attorneys, judges, and probation officers specialize in certain phases of the criminal justice procedure, whereas the prosecutor's responsibilities cross all these domains, making this the only official to work daily with all the practitioners of the criminal justice system. Those of you who are interning in the court system will have the opportunity to observe the powers of the prosecutor. These powers will become evident when the prosecutor uses his or her discretion to determine which defendants are to be prosecuted, the type of pleas to be bargained, and the severity of sentencing.

Defense attorneys share their discretionary powers with their clients. Although they may use their discretionary powers to decide whether to accept cases (private or court referred) or how much time to invest in cases, other decisions must be made with the defendants, such as what motions to file, what pleas to enter, and whether to plea-bargain. Because plea-bargaining is attributed to most of the guilty pleas in the United States, some practitioners consider it a form of discretion involving the defendant, the defense attorney, the prosecutor, and occasionally, the judge. However, most people are so intimidated by the legal process that they frequently give up their discretion and allow their defense attorneys to exercise complete discretion.

Gifis (1978) reported that *correctional officials* also frequently utilize discretion through differential treatment of institutionalized criminals. Among other things, they can decide whether to ignore or report an incident to the warden. Probation and parole officers, as extensions of correctional officers, also exercise a great deal of discretion in their capacity, to decide how strictly to enforce the conditions of probation or parole, including whether to allow individuals to travel or relocate outside the state. Juvenile probation officers even have the discretion to decide whether a probationer can marry, travel or relocate, or join the armed forces (Cox and Wade, 1998). Although there is much controversy regarding the types and use of discretion, practitioners believe that the function of discretion at all levels of the criminal justice system is invaluable. During your internship, be aware of how the political process operates and the impact of bureaucracy on your agency's performance.

FINANCE AND POLITICS

Financial considerations, which are also influenced by politics, play a crucial role in agencies' acquisition and allocation of financial resources. Most criminal justice agencies are funded by tax dollars. Although some agencies receive federal funds, the majority receive local and state funds. Presently, federal assistance to local and state agencies is at an all-time low, which has forced local and state governments to seek new avenues of funding for their criminal justice agencies. In most agencies, employees' salaries and benefit packages receive the highest financial consideration. As of late, all three levels of government have been more careful and creative in managing their financial resources, particularly in the field of corrections, where the trend is toward privatizing prisons. Furthermore, "between 1987 and 1993, state spending increases for corrections outpaced higher education by 41 percent nationwide" (Walters, 1995, p. 10).

Managing the budget is the most important daily function of an agency. A budget is a strategy to determine the agency's financial management based on anticipated income. Not only is it necessary to know the daily operating expenses, it is also important to be able to project the income required for future years of operation.

An agency's budget must be prepared in either of three ways: as a line-item budget, a planned program budget, or a zero-based budget. For a *line-item budget*, each unit of the agency is designated a line and shows customary costs, which can be used to compare from one fiscal year to the next. (See Figure 4.1 for a sample of a line-item budget.) The fiscal year may not always be the regular calendar year; for example, the fiscal year for your agency may be from October 1 to September 30 instead of January 1 to December 31 as is the calendar year. A *planned program budget* is more complex; each agency area is examined in terms of designated operational goals; then the manager of each area has to justify present and future expenses based on the methods used to achieve the operational goals. (See Figure 4.2 for an example of a planned program budget.) A *zero-based budget* is even more difficult. In zero-based budgeting, a completely new budget is adapted annually. The area managers must justify all expenses and the need for the services that are rendered.

Number of Placements		782
Line Item Description	%	Total
Contract Period	07/01/00-06/30/01	
Executive Director	100.00%	69,000.00
Project Director	100.00%	38,487.00
Training Specialist	100.00%	44,415.00
Accountant	100.00%	42,298.00
Administrative Assistant	100.00%	21,500.00
Program Assistant	100.00%	20,540.00
Program Assistant	100.00%	18,290.00
Program Assistant	100.00%	15,300.00
Case Manager/Trainer	100.00%	29,500.00
Job Developer/Counselor	100.00%	29,460.00
Job Developer/Counselor	100.00%	27,300.00
Job Developer/Counselor	100.00%	26,498.00
Job Developer/Counselor	100.00%	26,015.00
Job Developer/Counselor	100.00%	25,200.00
Job Developer/Counselor	100.00%	23,415.00
Counselor (Summer Youth)	100.00%	3,987.00
Total	100.00%	461,205.00
002	Participants' Wages	100%	18,350.00
003	Participants' FICA	100%	1,459.00
004	Participants' Workcomp	100%	250.00
006	Client Transport SYETP	100%	2,350.00
101	Staff Salaries	100%	461,205.00
200	Staff MICA (Medicare)	100%	7,230.00
201	Staff FICA (Social Security)	100%	27,545.00
202	Staff Worker's Compensation	100%	7,020.00
203	Staff Unemployment	100%	4,860.00
204	Staff Group Ins.	100%	35,100.00
205	Staff Group Life Ins.	100%	1,820.00
240	Gen'l Adm. Overhead	100%	37,300.00
000	Courier Services	100%	792.00
252	Audit Cost	100%	9,650.00
301	Gen Liability Insurance	100%	2,450.00
303	Bonding	100%	650.00
304	Other Insurance (Flood)	100%	202.00
350	Telephone-Local	100%	5,000.00
350	Telephone-Long Distance	100%	2,000.00
360	Electrical Services	100%	4,998.00
410	Equipment Repair & Maintenance	100%	3,549.00
411	Bldg. Maint-Janitor	100%	3,350.00

Figure 4.1   Miami Criminal Justice Agency Line-Item Budget

Number of Placements		782
Line Item Description	%	Total
Contract Period	07/01/00-06/30/01	
415　Confer & Prof Meeting	100%	700.00
450　Equipment Rental(copier, computer, phone)	100%	9,897.00
460　Space Rental	100%	19,500.00
501　Postage	100%	13,000.00
502　Printing	100%	4,000.00
503　Publications Books	100%	300.00
504　Advertising	100%	350.00
507　Membership	100%	1,575.00
510　Local Travel Reimb.	100%	20,992.00
521　Office Supplies	100%	5,140.00
522　Special Client Supplies	100%	615.00
527　Supportive Service	100%	5,540.00
530　Client Services	100%	2,575.00
542　Tuition & Books	100%	7,080.00
600　OJT Wages (Participants)	100%	10,050.00
TOTAL	100%	738,444.00

Figure 4.1　(Cont.)

With all three types of budgets, all the managers prepare budgets for their areas or departments and send them to the agency's financial representative, who prepares submissions forms for the budgetary items. The financial representative then sends these forms to the committee of the state legislature that is responsible for budgetary matters. The committee members review and edit these budgetary items and accept the agency's budget, which is voted on by the entire legislature. If the budget is approved, expenditures are allocated, and periodic audits are conducted.

The line-item budget is popular in criminal justice agencies. The budget shown in Figure 4.1 is a line-item budget for a Miami agency whose main mission is to assist ex-convicts in their transition from prison to society. Because there is no explanation of expenditures, it is considered an open-ended budget in that the agency director is requesting funds for services performed or needed with no justification. The budget shown in Figure 4.2 is a planned program budget for the Florida Department of Corrections. With this type of budget, each service is measured and justified.

During your internship, it may or may not become obvious to you that your agency is constantly confronted with monetary and budgeting issues. After observing the situation for a while, ask your supervisor to give you some insight into the

Department of Corrections
Budget Summary
(FY 2000-01)

OPERATING FUNDS
Expenditures by Budget Entity:

Department Administration	$ 62,746,451
Custody and Control	$ 1,039,643,013
Health Services	$ 246,174,629
Community Supervision	$ 229,093,922
Programs	$ 59,041,344
TOTAL OPERATING FUNDS	$ 1,636,699,359

FIXED CAPITAL OUTLAY FUNDS
EXPENDITURES BY PROJECT CLASSIFICATION

To provide additional capacity through expansion & new construction	$ 31,378,644
To maintain existing facilities and meet requirements of regulatory agencies	$ 16,210,319
TOTAL FIXED CAPITAL OUTLAYS	$ 47,588,953
TOTAL	$ 1,658,319,871

LOCAL FUNDS VOLUME OF COLLECTION ACTIVITIES:

Cost of Supervision Fees	$ 26,523,265
Restitution, Fines, and Court Costs	$ 49,891,401
Subsistence, Transportation, and other Court-Ordered Payments	$ 17,268,576

INMATE BANKING ACTIVITIES:

Total Deposits	$ 68,032,311
Total Disbursements	$ 71,131,462
June 30, 2001 Total Assets	$ 7,773,687

INMATE WELFARE FUND ACTIVITY:

Merchandise Sales	$ 35,970,851
Gross Profit From Sales	$ 13,259,722
Inmate Telephone Commissions	$ 16,027,174
June 30, 2001 Retained Earnings	$ 20,444,174

Source: Florida Department of Corrections*2000–01 Annual Report

Figure 4.2   Sample Planned Program Budget

agency's budget and the effects of bureaucracy on the agency's acquisition and allocation of funds. Whereas several of my interns have been employed by agencies after interning, others could not be hired because of "freezes" on hiring owing to reduced federal or state funding to these agencies. All these issues will become clearer once you understand the type of budget under which your agency is operating.

THE AGENCY'S CONSTITUTIONAL JUSTIFICATION

Just as you should be informed about your agency's budget, you should also be aware of the constitutional justification for your agency. At the beginning of your internship, it is appropriate to request a copy of the agency's mission statement and laws that are applicable to implementing the mission. As is discussed in criminal justice courses, the legal bases for all criminal justice agencies can be found in various laws and statutes, as well as in recent court rulings and executive decisions by the three levels of government. (See Box 4.1 for the legal justification for the creation of the California Department of the Youth Authority and information on the department's vision, mission statement, and priorities.) All criminal justice agencies have a legal basis, even if they operate in the private sector, such as the organization mentioned in Figure 4.1. All law enforcement agencies; local and state courts; and county sheriffs', district attorneys', and justices of the peace officers are constitutionally authorized agencies. Many state constitutions also allow communities to establish local law enforcement agencies and courts if they are deemed necessary.

Mandated laws at all levels of government grant constitutional justification for the establishment of most criminal justice agencies and for the reorganization and redirection of various agencies and programs. A case in point is the recent revamping of Florida's juvenile justice system.

Prior to 1994 the Department of Juvenile Justice was under the auspices of the Florida Department of Health and Rehabilitative Services (HRS), a social service organization. Under the direction of HRS, the juvenile justice system was constantly under attack by the public and the media. In 1989 a task force was formed to examine and evaluate programs in other states, in 1990 the task force's recommendations were accepted, and in 1994 House Bill 1927 was passed, creating a new director of juvenile justice in the state of Florida. This is a good example of legislative powers at work and proof of the constitutional justification of this system (Florida Department of Corrections, 1995–1996).

During classroom discussions, my students have found the historical reviews (which are necessary for their term papers) of their agencies fascinating. Although they were familiar with several of the internship agencies and knew that all were established for particular reasons, they were surprised to learn that the present function of many of these has changed over the years. For example, the Secret Service, which is thought of mainly as a protection service for the president, his staff, and other domestic and foreign dignitaries, was founded in 1865 to protect U.S. interest in the integrity of its currency; in other words, counterfeiting was of great concern then, as it is today. However, the responsibilities of the Secret Service have increased tremendously over the years.

Other federal organizations, such as the Federal Bureau of Investigation and the Bureau of Alcohol, Tobacco, and Firearms, were established by acts of Congress. In the event that your agency supervisor and other staff members are not

BOX 4.1   *Historical Overview of the California Department of the Youth Authority*

History

The California Department of the Youth Authority (CYA) was created by law in 1941, but it wasn't until 1943 that the agency began to operate "reform schools," providing institutional training and parole supervision for juveniles and young offenders. It is the largest offender agency in the nation, with more than 5,700 young men and women in institutions and camps and approximately 4,200 more on parole.

As a part of the state's juvenile justice system, the CYA works closely with law enforcement, the courts, prosecutors, probation, and a broad spectrum of public and private agencies concerned with and involved in the problems of youth.

Mission

The California Department of the Youth Authority's mission, as described in Section 1700 of the Welfare and Institutions Code, is to protect the public from criminal activity. The law mandates that department to:

- Provide a range of education, treatment, and training services for youthful offenders committed by the courts.
- Direct these offenders to participate in community and victim restoration.
- Assist local justice agencies with efforts to control crime and delinquency.
- Encourage the development of state and local programs to prevent crime and delinquency.

The CYA is a department in the Youth and Adult Correctional Agency, whose Secretary reports directly to the Governor and serves on his Cabinet.

Important activities having to do with legislation, legal affairs, labor relations, program compliance, equal employment opportunity, technology, systems review, and public affairs/public information are carried out by the Office of the Director.

The CYA carries out its responsibilities through five administrative branches—*Prevention and Victim Services, Institutions and Camps, Education Services, Parole Services and Community Corrections,* and *Administrative Services.*

> The CYA receives its youthful offender population from both juvenile and criminal court referrals, and offenders committed directly to the CYA do not receive determinate sentences. The Youthful Offender Parole Board, a separate administrative body, determines their parole release. Those committed by the criminal courts who cannot complete their sentence by age 21 are transferred to the Department of Correction (CDC) prisons at age 18.
>
> In practice, the period of incarceration is determined by the severity of the committed offense and the offender's progress toward parole readiness. The incarceration time may not exceed the limits of determinate sentences for adults committing the same crime.
>
> In addition, the CYA's jurisdiction for the most serious felony offenders, both juvenile and young adults ends on the offender's 25th birthday (California Youth Authority, 2003).

aware of the judicial acts relative to the agency (which some of my students have found to be the case), you may want to do this research on your own.

OVERSEEING FIELD-PLACEMENT AGENCIES

How are organizations and their employees made accountable for protecting the liberties of the public? In addition to politics and laws discussed previously, there is added protection from citizens themselves, the media, and the civil liberties organizations.

There is no question about the power of the people, as addressed in the section on discretion. With the advent of new technology, especially the Internet, it is more convenient for the general public to be more readily informed regarding local and national cover-ups, as well as other issues related to the criminal justice system. The media, both print and electronic, certainly provide more news information services. If one chooses to become personally involved, one only has to tune in to CNN, FOX, or MSNBC, among other news programs, for constant minute-by-minute news coverage and opportunities. Newspapers and magazines certainly also play an enormous role in policing criminal justice agencies and the conduct of their employees. Since the Civil Rights Act of 1964, numerous lawsuits have been filed over discrimination, brutality, and negligence by administrative officials. All these external checks are crucial to protecting the rights of all members of society.

STATED OPERATIVE GOALS

An understanding of your agency's behavior requires a close examination of the goals indicated in its operating procedures. This chapter provides information that will help you to understand the various types of organizational goals that are important to the daily functioning of an agency.

The major categories of organizational goals that are usually discussed are official and operative goals. According to Perrow (1961), *official goals* are the general purposes of the organization, as declared by its charter, mission statement, and bureaucratic pronouncements, whereas *operative goals* are the policies that determine the actual behavior of the organization. The operative goals, standards by which daily decisions are made by agency personnel, are more relevant to understanding organizational behavior and may be different from the official goals. For example, the official goal of a police department may be to create a secure environment in the community that will enhance the quality of the citizens' lives. The official goal of the Department of Corrections may be to provide programs and services to offenders and to supervise offenders at the level of security comparable with the danger they present. These official goals are ambiguous, and as Perrow (1961) stated, they do not reflect the operative goals of political groups in organizations, decision making and competition among these groups, and the accessibility of resources.

The purpose of the goals of criminal justice agencies is to specify procedures for daily management. As discussed earlier, the establishment of agencies' official and operative goals is influenced by political, financial, and judicial considerations. An agency's traditional precedent, for example, its mission (the agency has always rendered a specific service), may also be an influence.

For organizations that are sponsored by governmental agencies, such as juvenile and adult corrections agencies, the authority for setting official goals, rules, and regulations and the procurement of capital and operating expenses lies with governmental officials appointed by political committees. The enormity of the organizations, the complicated procedures for accountability, and the pressures associated with the tenuous relationship with the political committees indicate the importance of the administrative functions. Professional influence is also increasing in these organizations, and professional groups are beginning to make a considerable impact on some components of the criminal justice system. These professionals may assume control of various organizations or may be instrumental in hiring administrators who are committed to achieving the organizations' positive goals, such as the rehabilitation of clients, as has occurred in a few federal penal institutions (privatization) and a few state juvenile correctional institutions (boot camps). These are good examples of the influence of operative goals.

The Federal Bureau of Prisons set six official goals for 1995 and beyond. It proposed to do the following:

1. Proactively manage its offender population to ensure safe and secure operations.
2. Have a competent and representative workforce meeting the organization's needs up to and beyond the year 2000.

3. Maintain its facilities in operationally sound condition and in compliance with security, safety, and environmental requirements.

4. Manage its operation and resources in a competent and effective manner which encourages creativity and innovation in development of exemplary programs as well as excellence in maintaining the basics of correctional management. The bureau continually strives toward improvements in its effective use of resources and its efficient delivery of services.

5. Provide services and programs to address inmate needs, providing productive use-of-time activities, and facilitating the successful reintegration of inmates into society, consistent with community expectations and standards.

6. Continue to seek opportunities for expanding the involvement of community, and local, state, and federal agencies. (U.S. Department of Justice, 1995, pp. 1–12).

These are the official goals for the Bureau of Prisons provided by the U.S. Department of Justice. However, an intern working with the Bureau of Prisons reported that several operative goals have been established at her office to realize the bureau's official goals:

- Secure a new contract for a halfway house with the capacity to house 75 inmates.
- Update the computer system to enhance productivity.
- Remodel the third floor to provide office space for the community corrections administrator.
- Recruit new interns to assist in the daily operations of the office.

Are these operational goals reflective of the agency's official goals? Generally, they are. Are those of you who are presently interning aware of the official goals of your agencies? Have you been able to observe any significant difference between official and operative goals? For those of you who are just starting your internships, it is recommended that you request a copy of your agencies' official goals; inquire how, why, and by whom these particular goals were established; and note the difference between how these two sets of goals are operationalized.

During your internship, you may discover that the organization's official goals are not considered in the operative goals or that the official goals have been completely altered, a phenomenon called *goal displacement* (Gordon and McBride, 1990). Although goal displacement occurs in several criminal justice agencies, it is nearly impossible for it to occur in others.

A good example of goal displacement occurred in an agency of which I am a board member. The original official goals were to assist adult inmates in the transition from prison into society. Over the years, federal funding diminished in this area; thus, in 1996, the agency began to consider extending its services to juveniles. Today, the agency provides services to both adults and youthful offenders. In this case, goal displacement enabled the agency to maintain its organizational structure, acquire fiscal resources, preserve its public image, and retain its staff. Not only was the agency rescued by changing its official goals, but it was able to extend its scope and make an even greater contribution to the community.

The following are accounts from two interns who reported that it is impossible for goal displacement to occur in their internship agencies. The first intern reported:

> At the Federal Bureau of Prisons our goals are dictated by statute. . . . We have a distinct mission and are held accountable for everything we do. . . . There is no room to be creative and develop our own plans; . . . the Government Accounting Office looks at all our expenditures, and we must spend our money in designated areas. (Bankston, 1997)

The other intern stated:

> The goals of the Guardian Ad Litem program revolve around the power of the lay guardians (GALs). All staff members are present to assist the lay guardians by informing them when and how to "obtain information and advocate for services." The staff members organize information, upgrade organizational capabilities, and monitor legislative efforts for the sole purpose of facilitating the objectives of the GALS. The GALS accept a case and are committed to fulfilling several official goals, with the support and supervision of the staff. These goals include: (1) to complete an intensive investigation of the case, (2) to report findings to the court, (3) to ensure representation of the children's best interests, (4) to monitor all proceedings and services relevant to the case, (5) to attend training, (6) to consult regularly with the supervisor in the particular division, (7) to participate in evaluations of your performance, and (8) to strive to attain permanency for the children at the earliest possible time. Operative goals of this agency fit these official goals well. That is, there is a very small discrepancy between the pursuit of these goals. Official goals are rigorously applied to everyday endeavors. (Santos, 1997)

Over the years, the interns in our program have asked to be placed in agencies whose work relates to their professional goals. It was also important to them that these agencies were not practicing goal displacement, which could prevent them from gaining experience in the types of agencies with the types of clients with whom they needed to work to accomplish their goals. For example, if an intern who wanted to work only with adults was placed in the agency described earlier (the coordinator being unaware of the goal displacement) and was required to work with juvenile delinquents, the experience could be unsatisfactory. If you are placed in an agency that is experiencing goal displacement and thus will be prevented from gaining experience in your chosen area, contact your coordinator as soon as possible and ask to be placed in another agency. This is not to imply that it is not good to work at an agency that is experiencing goal displacement; goal displacement is common in certain criminal justice agencies for various reasons, including those just stated. Interning at such an agency will be a problem for you only if it prevents you from receiving the experience you desire.

SOCIAL SYSTEMS GOALS

Social systems goals are related to an agency's contribution to the operation of a social system in which it is embedded (Perrow, 1961). For example, alternative schools for children who have been adjudicated delinquents by the juvenile courts are part of the school system. Organizations may perform accommodating, gratificatory, integrated, or model-maintenance functions (Parsons, 1951). For instance, Scott's (1959) study of prisons and mental hospitals reported that organizations serving integrative functions for the community will emphasize integrative functions in the organizations with which they are affiliated.

All four functions are considered important for an organization's survival, although they may be accomplished through different goals in different organizations. For example, the official goal of a police department may be to enforce laws, prevent crime, maintain order, and maintain positive police–community relations, whereas a criminal justice agency may include these four functions in its goals of providing institutional services (interviewing soon-to-be released inmates), services to clients (providing employment upon release), maintaining a professionally trained and managed organization, and proactively seeking ways to prevent recidivism by educating employers to accept and train ex-offenders.

AFFILIATIONS WITH AGENCY SYSTEMS

As earlier stated, most criminal justice agencies use a multisystems approach to accomplish their goals. Many agencies must be prepared to intervene with clients at a variety of systems levels, including individual, family, extended family, church, community, and social services. It would be impossible to describe this immensely complicated multisystem in a sketch of one organization because of the vast number and combinations of procedures in various parts of the country. Therefore, in this section a small-scale agency relationship chart for the Homestead Police Department is presented (see Figure 4.3), in addition to a description of the department's affiliations with other organizations.

The Homestead Police Department enforces federal and state laws in five patrol zones within a 13-square-mile area. The department's 72 officers provide assistance to approximately 27,000 residents. As indicated in Figure 4.3, the major social and educational agencies with which the police department is affiliated on a regular basis are the Department of Children and Family Services (CFS), Dade County Public Schools, Dade County Housing and Urban Development (HUD) Corporation, and other community programs. For example, one program, Project Start Off Smart (SOS), is a partnership program between the Homestead Police Department, Dade County Public Schools, and the CFS. The goal of SOS, created in 1991, is to stabilize the family unit, with the hope of reducing the number of interventions and eliminating the duplication of services by some agencies.

Figure 4.3   Homestead Police Department and Agency Affiliations

Referrals to the program are provided by police officers, school personnel, CFS, and the community. In 1995, the majority of the referrals (43%) were for domestic violence; the remainder were for child abuse and neglect and sexual abuse (30%), family services (AFDC, child custody, and substance abuse) (20%), and miscellaneous (such as services for the elderly and homeless persons) (7%).

The Drug Abuse Resistance Education (DARE) Program is an affiliation between the Homestead Police Department and the Dade County Public Schools. Police officers teach the program in two area elementary schools and take students on picnics and on bowling and swimming outings. Another affiliation involves two school resource officers, one who is assigned to one area middle school and the other who divides his time between the second area middle school and the senior high schools. These officers manage the Crossover Program, which is designed for students who are at risk of dropping out who are referred to the program by the juvenile court, the Juvenile Alternative Sanctioned System, Project SOS, CFS, and school administrators or by parents' requests. The goal of DARE is to reduce school truancy, dropout, and juvenile delinquency. A third affiliation between the police department and the schools is the Traffic Safety Officer Program, in which a police officer teaches youth occupant protection and awareness of "driving under the influence" (DUI) in all Homestead schools, from kindergarten through grade 12. The Youth Occupant Protection Program's curriculum consists of information on the leading causes of death and injury to young people from automobile and bicycle accidents.

In 1995, a short-term affiliation between the police department and HUD resulted in the Citizen Awareness Program, which introduced citizens to a wide range of crime-fighting techniques, from first aid to crime reporting. The program included eleven weeks of classroom training by visiting instructors and concluded with a field trip to the police station.

One community program, the Police Explorers, is provided by the Homestead Police Department in conjunction with the Boy Scouts of America for boys ages 14 to 21. These participants, called cadets, must complete an extensive training program in a curriculum that incorporates accepted police academy requirements. Upon graduation, these Police Explorers assist patrol officers at parades and other significant activities with crowd and traffic control. Some former Police Explorers have become certified police officers, and others are currently working in a civilian capacity for the Homestead Police Department (Homestead Police Department, 1995).

Along with these social and educational affiliations, the Homestead Police Department has the same systematic relationships with criminal justice agencies for the prosecution of criminal cases as do other police departments. These agencies include the State Police, the Sheriff's Department, and those discussed earlier: the Office of the State Attorney, the Public Defender's Office, the courts, the departments of probation and parole, and corrections agencies.

Although the relationships between criminal justice agencies and the Police Department are not shown in Figure 4.3, it is still evident that the multisystems are intricate for a relatively small neighborhood such as Homestead and that the department's affiliations with schools, social service agencies, and other community agencies are numerous. During your internship, you may discover that the relationships between your agency and others are different, as in the following example of a student's report of her agency's interaction with other agencies:

> The Family Intervention Specialty Program's (FISP) [a division of the Florida Department of Juvenile Justice] major problem is that FISP is forced to interact with many different organizations throughout the course of one day. Each of these organizations has its own rules and regulations. The problem is that the network that integrates the separate components of the criminal justice system is so fragmented that information does not flow smoothly. For instance, at FISP we have to contact a public school for information on a client. Then we may have to pull someone's records from the courts or from the police department. More often than not, the client lives in the Liberty Square Housing Project [so] HUD gets involved. If the family needs or is already receiving some sort of benefits, we usually have to contact CFS.
>
> Since our clients are "at risk," we deal with a lot of the alternative schools in the area. The structure of some of these schools is so littered with red tape that the schools are worse than some of the public schools. FISP must deal with all these organizations on a day-to-day basis and must also deal with the Department of Juvenile Justice. Because of time constraints, dealing with all these organizations in one day is a tremendous task in itself. Then there is the added fact that several of these organizations seem to have a problem surrendering information to anyone outside their organizations. (Henderson, 1995)

This and other problems caused the intern to become cynical about the relationship of her internship agency and other agencies. One situation that was especially upsetting to her was the replacement of FISP's official policy and initial mission, when founded in 1993, of rehabilitating youths and shielding them from the traumatic and stigmatizing experience of criminal court with the goals of 1995 legislation to "lock up young offenders and get tough on crime," which, she believed, has caused the program to be ineffective because it is operating under a philosophy for which it was not intended.

During your internship it is important to be aware that your perspective on particular criminal justice matters may be influenced by your agency's environment and to understand that other agencies' goals and responsibilities may be different. The affiliations will vary depending on the type of agency you are working in, the type of agencies that interact with your agency, and the contribution your agency wishes to make to the social system in which it is cradled.

SUMMARY

In this chapter we discussed the bureaucratic, financial, and judicial systems that affect your agency's performance. For interns in agencies in small communities, politics will play a different role than it will for interns in agencies located in large communities. Whereas the politics of small communities are controlled by families or groups, the politics of large communities are controlled by criminal justice special-interest groups. Bureaucracy, power, and authority are explicitly linked with the financial strategies of the agency. You may be able to witness this interaction at your internship placement by observing political alliances between your agency administrators and other criminal justice officials.

In reviewing the impact of the judicial system on your agency's operations, we introduced the authority associated with the power of discretion afforded the police, prosecutors, defense attorneys, judges, correctional officers, and the public (regarding citizens' decisions of whether to aid these officials in performing their duties).

As has been shown, it is crucial for agencies to be cost effective and otherwise to take monetary issues into consideration if they are to be allotted their necessary fiscal resources. State tax dollars support most criminal justice agencies, although some agencies, on occasion, obtain federal assistance. Management of the budget is considered the most significant daily operation of the agency. Although budgets are prepared either by line-item, planned program, or zero-based budgeting, criminal justice agencies mainly use line-item budgeting. Therefore, you should become familiar with this type of budget.

In addition, at the beginning of your internship, you should inquire about the constitutional justification of your agency. The legal basis for most criminal justice agencies can be found in various laws and statutes, recent court rulings, and executive decisions made by local, state, or federal governments. Again, you may want to research the statutory laws related to your agency. The chapter included a discussion of the parts that citizens, the media, and civil liberty organizations play in ensuring that the public's liberty is protected.

The discussion on agencies' goals and affiliations with social systems started by describing the difference between official and operative goals that function as rules and regulations for daily management and long-term strategies for most criminal justice organizations. It then pointed out that goal displacement is also associated with an agency's official and operative goals and can occur whenever the official goals are ignored or changed. Because most agencies work in partnership with other agencies, it is also important for them to develop social systems goals that will result in the provision of the best possible services for the community. The chapter ended with a discussion of agency affiliations in the criminal justice system. These relationships are often influenced by legal, economic, or political factors that result in administrative decisions that influence official and/or operative goals and may ultimately cause you or other agency personnel to become biased about the agency's role and affiliations with other organizations. In conclusion, in the criminal justice system, the community is always considered in the development of organizational goals, whether official or operational, and goal setting is considered an interactive process.

DISCUSSION QUESTIONS

1. What are the three systems that influence a student's particular agency? Be able to distinguish between the three.
2. How is bureaucracy linked with the financial strategies of a given agency?
3. What is the difference between official and operative goals? For a student, which is more important to be familiar with while involved in an internship?
4. When should an agency develop social systems goals?

Field-Placement Considerations

Now that you have selected your internship site, had your interview, and passed your background screening, it is time to consider what your role will be at your field placement. Your first consideration should be the available learning opportunities. Although your internship coordinator may have discussed these opportunities with you prior to placement, it is essential for you to be clear about what the agency supervisor expects of you. It is also important for the agency supervisor to be aware of what you expect to learn from your field education. No matter how exciting the placement may sound (like the Secret Service), the lack of interesting and challenging educational opportunities can result in a negative experience. It is important that you are not used as a gofer or file clerk, and it is your responsibility to clarify your role from the beginning. As an internship coordinator, I attempt to prevent or counteract any disappointments by discussing these issues before students are assigned to agencies and during site visits and by including them in the agency agreements.

Once the goals of the internship are clarified, you will begin learning by observing. It is your agency supervisor's responsibility to give you the opportunity to observe various components of the activities that occur in the agency—from clerical work to staff meetings to interactions with clients and any other pertinent services. Certainly, every element of an organization is not rewarding or fascinating, and you should be exposed to the boring as well as the exciting aspects of the placement.

On the basis of your training, once your agency supervisor thinks you are capable, you may move from observation to interaction. While your goals should include pursuing new challenges head on, considering your capabilities, your involvement in agency activities should still be closely supervised. For instance, if you have been a participant-observer in a courtroom for several weeks, your supervising attorney may allow you to try your hand at writing or helping to write legal briefs. Or, if you have observed a therapy group for several weeks, you may be asked to co-facilitate it, as well as to record your observations. Finally, you should ask your agency supervisor to give you specific information regarding the agency's policies, rules, and regulations and base your conduct and actions on them. In Chapter 5 we discuss your role as an intern. Chapter 6 will enhance your understanding of the role your agency, agency supervisor, internship coordinator, and faculty supervisor play in your internship experience. In Chapter 7 we explain ethical standards for criminal justice professionals.

5

The Intern's Role

How do you see your role as an intern?
Do you have good observational and writing skills?
Are you comfortable asking questions?

ORIENTATION

The agency staff will have been informed of your day of arrival and will have established a working assignment. In initially addressing your role as an intern, your agency supervisor's discussion of personnel practices may well include working hours, work breaks (if any), personal conduct, procedures and routines, appropriate dress (if not discussed during the interview), confidentiality of information, and any other pertinent information.

Suelzle and Borzak (1981) suggested that the roles of interns change as interns progress through a series of stages. According to these researchers, the orientation process takes place during the intern's "initial entry" stage. In this stage you will probably be both excited and anxious about the internship. The question of acceptance will be utmost in your mind.

After the orientation period, you will no longer be treated as a visitor. Your role as an intern will fall somewhere between that of a student and a professional. There will still be many tasks for you to learn, but you may also be perceived as a knowledgeable person with some skills. Keep in mind that most agencies and staff view the internship as a means of contributing to the development of young professionals, showing an ongoing commitment to the development of the profession, obtaining new input from students, providing the enriching experience of supervision to senior staff, and gaining local and national recognition.

Upon considering your experience and training, your agency supervisor may gradually increase your responsibilities. You may be encouraged to observe situations and attend staff meetings that only agency personnel usually attend. During such meetings and observations, some agency personnel may accept you and be friendly toward you, but others may not. The ambivalence they exhibit reflects their confusion about who you are and the purpose of your internship. Furthermore, the invitation to attend these functions by no means implies that your position is equal to that of a staff person, only that you are being permitted to observe another facet of the agency's operations.

The staff's reactions to you may depend a great deal on the precedents set by previous interns and whether the staff sees you as a threat. They will probably compare you to previous interns. Interns who have created a positive impression will have left high standards for you to emulate, whereas those who did not will have created a negative impression for you to counteract. During this phase, which is referred to as *probationary*, you may sometimes be judged by unfair standards that have nothing to do with your abilities and over which you have no control. However, you do have control over your ultimate evaluation, after *your* performance has been evaluated. Throughout this period, you should follow two easy rules: (1) Be honest with yourself and with others, and (2) do your best (Baird, 1996, p. 19). Remember that as a student intern, your goal is to learn. Do not be afraid to ask questions or to say you do not know an answer to a question. The best way to reduce pressure and help yourself do your best is to be honest about your limitations. This attitude will also guarantee that you have a much more fulfilling and inspiring internship.

Participant Observation

The moment you walk into the agency, your role as a participant observer begins. You immediately begin to study your surroundings, including the people and the activities that are occurring. In the agency you will be much more aware of this process than you are in other areas of your life, including the classroom, because your new responsibilities will make you more conscious of your observational role.

This type of observation requires more skills because you eventually have to record and report what you have seen and done. In most internship courses, as in mine, you are required to write an observation/participation paper that you submit at the end of the internship. Your observations in the agency will afford you the opportunity to enhance your mental note-taking skills until such time as you are able to record the significant events of each day. To keep track of these events and activities, it is helpful for you to maintain a journal, since experience in recording will help you hone the skills you need to describe and assess your internship experience. Although you may initially record everything, you will eventually need to distinguish what is important from what is insignificant. In some organizations you may be assigned to various departments for short periods to give you an idea of all their functions. My students who intern at the Secret Service, for example, spend some time in protection (guarding the president and other prominent dignitaries), some time in detecting counterfeit money, and some time in other areas. Students interning with the Office of the State Attorney must choose between working as law clerks, domestic abuse case interviewers, criminal intake counselors, or victim/witness advocates. In such cases, you ultimately have to decide which facet of the organization you want to observe in depth and ask to be assigned to that department. You will probably pay more attention to an area that is compatible with the goals you and your supervisor have determined and that are influenced by the job or jobs you actually perform at your placement.

Once you have decided in which area you are interested, you will be ready to document your daily or weekly experiences.

The following questions provide a good benchmark to use in documenting your observation participation experiences:

Who are you observing? (gender, ethnicity, age, background, individual, group, etc.)

What are you observing? (activities, happenings, situation, people, event, milieu, etc.)

Where are you observing? (formal or informal environment, location, date, physical environment, etc.)

When are you observing? (time of day, sequence of events, before or after relevant event, response, reaction, etc.)

How are you observing? (complete participant, complete observer, natural or structured environment, expectations, hypothesis, culturally relevant/irrelevant lens, context, etc.)

Why are you observing? (classification, social issues, journal entry, date collection, etc.)

By using this critical thinking approach to your participant observation, you can maintain a level of objectivity and get the most pertinent information. This will be necessary throughout the internship.

DATA COLLECTION METHODS

There are several ways to collect data. As I just mentioned, I encourage you to do so by keeping a journal. Entering your thoughts and impressions each day will not only ensure that the information is accurate and up to date, but it will give you valuable experience that will enhance your sense of self-reflection and note-taking skills. The following is an example of a journal entry:

Thursday, April 10, 1997
11:00–12:30

Met with Ms. Ferrell (supervisor) and followed up on yesterday's implementation of improvement priorities program. Agreed that Goal 1, readiness to start class, was achieved. We will discuss a time line for implementing Goal 2 during tomorrow's meeting. Also spoke with Joy regarding transportation to her juvenile court hearing next Tuesday. Received permission to accompany Joy to court. Will report back to Ms. Ferrel regarding the disposition of the hearing during staff meeting on Friday.

12:30–1:00

Lunch in the cafeteria. Was introduced to two students who were experiencing their first day in an alternative school setting. They both were nervous and were looking forward to the end of the school day.

1:00–2:00

Provided tutoring for two new students. Both students seemed to enjoy the special attention for a brief period and then became very distracted. Discussed situation with supervisor and submitted a brief report for the students' records.

The journal should be used to record your daily experiences at your placement. In these journal entries it is beneficial to include your personal reactions to situations, thoughts about staff or clients, and impressions of procedures or treatments and the formal or informal atmosphere of the organization. Take notes on ideas and projects that pique your curiosity so that you can discuss them with your agency supervisor at a later time. It is essential that you maintain confidentiality when you write or discuss any entry by using fictitious names or only first names when referring to clients. A chronological format, in which you indicate the day, data, and hour of activities or events; information on clients; activities; and staff involvement will be beneficial for updating your internship coordinator on your daily activities; reporting the hours you spent at the agency; and when applicable, preparing your term paper.

Starting a Journal

To record your initial impressions of the agency and its personnel, you need to decide which recording method you want to use before you begin the internship. Your first impressions of your placement are important because the first day is the only time you will be able to view the agency as a member of the community rather than as part of the organization. Furthermore, these initial impressions will come in handy when you compare them to what you have learned at the end of the placement.

Although you will eventually decide the specific areas you want to record, it is not necessary to do so during the first week. Relax and record your observations at random, without any particular focus. Later, when you are more at ease with your surroundings and the staff members, you will become aware of your specific areas of interest.

The first things you may want to include, which some of my students have done, are descriptions of the environment and whether the structure is formal or informal. Then you may want to add demographic information on the agency personnel (their ages, racial and ethnic backgrounds, and genders) and alliances (cliques) among the staff. You may want to include information on agency space allocation, the arrangement of furniture in the reception areas and offices, and how the walls are decorated. You may want to add information on how the staff dress (such as casual or business attire). Finally, you may want to include how the agency staff relate to clients, how clients respond to staff, and your impression of the relationship between the agency and the community.

When your placement environment becomes more comfortable and your observations are more perceptive, it is a good idea to begin to compare classroom theory with actual practice. During this process you may find that you either refine or reject your initial ideas and concepts on the basis of your experience in the agency.

Planning Interviews

In collecting data and recording observations for the required term paper, my students interview staff members and clients (when appropriate) to help them understand better the key issues and problems associated with the agency. Before you schedule interviews with staff and clients, you should have a good idea what your focus will be in collecting and recording this information. In my opinion, recording your interviews is the best way to analyze various people's viewpoints, understanding, and positions.

To ensure that the interviews are successful, first decide on your area of interest (what you want to pursue in the interviews). Then schedule interviews with a few staff members (and clients, when permitted) who have specific knowledge of the particular area that is the most intriguing to you. You should be selective in your choice of interviewees, picking those who you think will best provide the information you need for your term paper and who are the most knowledgeable about your area of interest. Your agency supervisor can be helpful by directing you to willing and cooperative staff members and clients.

Preparing the Interview Guide

The next step is to prepare an interview guide. Serious thought should go into the production of your guide. The best way to begin is to think about things that may be puzzling to you. In quiet, reflective times during journal writing, ask yourself: "Am I feeling uncertain or confused about any aspect of the internship?" If so, begin to record relevant questions whenever these feelings of uncertainties occur. It is a good habit to have paper and pencil available at all times. I even keep a pad and pencil at my bedside for the occasions when I awake with a thought I may want to investigate in the morning. You will find that questions and thoughts arise at strange times, such as while you are riding in a bus, speaking with a friend, or watching television. Therefore, keeping a notebook handy can be advantageous.

Once you have refined your area of interest and sorted out what puzzles you, you are ready to draft a list of standard questions for the interviews. These standard questions will guarantee that each person you interview will be probed in a comparable manner. The sequence in which you conduct the interviews does not matter; what is important is that you cover every topic you have listed during the interview.

It is helpful for your interview guide to begin with a *face sheet* that covers the social characteristics of the interviewees. Although items for the face sheet vary, some of the most common are the person's name (or code number, if confidentiality is an issue), gender, age, education, race or ethnicity, residence (confidential in most law enforcement agencies), place and date of birth, and occupation, as well as the date and location of the interviews. Some of these items may be eliminated or additional items may be used, depending on the intentions of the interview. It is important to note that even though the face sheet is usually the first page, the questions on it are not always the initial ones that are asked. The topic, the level of trust that you and the interviewee have established, and other issues may influence whether you start at the face sheet or go directly into the interview. If you do the latter, you should eventually complete the face sheet for identification purposes.

During the interview, the emphasis should be on obtaining descriptions on or narratives of the person's feelings and thoughts. Therefore, it is preferable to compose open-ended questions. An example of an open-ended question is: "How do you feel about the working environment here?" This type of question allows the person to share his or her feelings on every aspect of the agency (if time permits). In contrast, a closed-end question such as "Is this a comfortable working environment for you?" may solicit a short and direct answer such as *yes* or *no*. If the person gives such an answer, you can follow up with a more direct question.

During the interview you should pay attention not only to what the person is saying, but to what he or she is not saying or is intimating through body language that you may consider significant. If this is your first experience with interviewing, I suggest that you first practice with friends and family members. The more you practice, the more comfortable you will feel during the actual interview.

Approaching Potential Interviewees

Once you have decided who you want to interview, contact each person individually to apprise him or her honestly and precisely of what you plan to cover in the interview and of how the interview will be conducted. All interviews should be conducted in the presence of your agency supervisor or assigned personel. As a courtesy, you should explain the purpose of the interview and the criteria for the selection process. Finally, tell the potential interviewees about your background and what stimulated your curiosity regarding the area of concern. It is easier to establish trust if you share something about yourself with them.

Two other important issues to address are confidentiality and tape recording. First, you should assure the interviewees that their names will not be used and that their answers will remain confidential. However, advise them that it is your duty to report any illegal behavior, so they should be cautious about admitting to this type of behavior. Second, if you plan to audiotape the interviews, ask the interviewees' permission beforehand and explain why you wish to do so.

Audio- and Videotaping Interviews

It is important to tape-record interviews because it is difficult to be attentive to everything an interviewee is saying if you are constantly writing. You must concentrate totally on the interview in a way that conveys that you are truly listening. However, do not fall into the trap of not listening to the interviewee because you think you will be able to catch everything later while listening to the tape. For example, tapes can be garbled, the interviewee may perceive that you are not truly interested, or you may miss subtle nuances of expression. Occasional note taking, such as writing key words or phrases, is a good method of combating this tendency.

If a person does not want to be audiotaped, you will have to rely on your note-taking and recall skills. Note taking is a process of keeping in touch with what is going on in an interview. As Lofland and Lofland (1984, p. 61) noted: "You take notes on what has already gone on, and notes on what should go on—what has now come up that you should ask about before the interview is over." Make sure that you write up your notes or transcripts of audiotaped interviews immediately after the interviews while the information is fresh in your mind to ensure that you are recording the most recent views and ideas.

In some agencies you will be given access to clients' files. While you are privy to this personal information, the issue of *confidentiality* should be constantly in your thoughts. It is important to learn with whom you are at liberty to discuss the contents of the files in the agency. The background information contained in the files may be invaluable in assisting you to develop an outline for your area of interest.

SELECTING, DESIGNATING, AND CHANGING AN INTERNSHIP

Internship coordinators have many factors to consider when matching students with agency supervisors. The first factor should be a student's preference. Sometimes, however, it may not be possible to do so, as when there are more requests for a placement than the agency supervisor can adequately supervise. For example, in my program, the Secret Service will only take two interns per semester from each neighboring college and university. This placement is so popular that I have to reserve placements a year in advance. Thus, if students want to work at this agency, they must apply in their junior year to be considered for placement in their senior year. The Secret Service also requires a lengthy background check that takes two to three months.

The second factor is a student's skill-development needs. It is important for your internship coordinator to match your skill level with the appropriate agency supervisor. For instance, if you need a structured environment to assist you in developing organizational skills, it will be helpful for you to be assigned to a supervisor who has time for a daily, one-on-one relationship. If you happen to have low self-confidence, you should be placed with a supervisor who can be patient and supportive of you. Although it is not always possible to make a perfect match, your internship coordinator can provide the best possible match based on both your and the agency supervisor's personality characteristics because of his or her relationship over time with various agency supervisors.

It is essential for you and your internship coordinator to establish a communication pattern, either by in-person meetings or telephone conferences. For small internship classes (less than 20 students), biweekly telephone conferences are recommended. I have found that within two weeks, my interns and the agency supervisors know whether there has been a positive match. If not, there is still ample time to relocate the intern with enough hours left to have a meaningful experience with a new agency.

As internship supervisor, I request a midterm evaluation from the agency supervisor, which requires a mid-internship meeting between the student and agency supervisor, during which the student's experience and performance up to that time are assessed and goals are set for the remaining time. During this meeting, it is also appropriate for you to address any concerns or problems that you have been experiencing with your agency supervisor and internship coordinator. In addition, it is important for you to tell your internship coordinator about any problems you are having with the agency supervisor in case these problems result in a negative evaluation. The internship coordinator needs this information to evaluate whether this is a favorable placement for professional and personal development and to determine if the site should be used in the future. See Chapter 8 for further discussion.

Whereas most internship placements are positive, you may not have a good relationship with your agency supervisor for various reasons, such as personnel problems, unforeseen crises, or other personal issues. If you encounter inadequate supervision for any reason, get in touch with your internship coordinator immediately for assistance in either transferring supervision within the agency or, if it is early enough in the semester, to find a new agency and supervisor.

PEER SUPPORT

In addition to the major roles played by your internship coordinator and agency supervisor in the success of your internship experience, your peers who are taking the same internship course or who have taken it previously may provide tremendous support. For example, they may be able to recommend potential sites or warn you against others (bearing in mind that you should consider this information carefully—people can view the same experience differently). If one of your peers confides that the placement only offered clerical work with little staff and no client contact, you may want to question the limitations of the learning opportunity provided by that agency.

Peers who share the same placement can also provide a feeling of comradeship. Although your internship coordinator and agency supervisor may try to relate to you and give you support, your peers are likely to share the same feelings of being overwhelmed, anxious, and incompetent and to listen to your feelings and concerns. Once you establish a bond with them, your feeling of being alone is usually diminished, you can learn how they are coping, and it becomes easier to work through this period.

Some criminal justice agencies function differently from others, depending on their locations. For instance, a police department in a rural area functions differently from one in an urban or suburban area. The differences among these locations may be apparent in their managerial styles, communication techniques, and agency interactions. If any of your peers have completed internship courses in these different settings, they can give you significant information that can help you decide where you want to work.

It may not always be possible for you and your peers to have a reciprocal supporting relationship. Therefore, it is important for you to realize and accept that there will be times when you may not be able to help each other. When circumstances dictate, advise your peer to consult with the agency supervisor or internship coordinator, and you do the same.

Peer support may be provided in ways other than dealing with crises. You may schedule periodic meetings during agency break times or plan outside activities to provide support on a regular basis. Also, your internship coordinator may do as I do and schedule three seminars a semester that allow time for peer discussions and support.

CASE STUDIES: STUDENT NARRATIVES

The following student narratives are taken from a series of observation participation term papers completed in April 2003.

The following statement is from a student interning at the Miami Halfway House, a moderate risk (Level 6) residential program for male juvenile offenders.

> Having the opportunity to intern at the Miami Halfway House allowed me not only to do intensive observation of the staff and offenders, but it also allowed me to assess whether I would consider a career in the juvenile justice system.
>
> In my role of intern at the Miami Halfway House (MHH), there were multiple goals I sought to accomplish in the specific areas of accumulating information, individual development, and educational/professional growth as mentioned in (Taylor, 1999, pp. 9–10). Accordingly, my goals were as follows:
>
> 1. I would like to achieve a better understanding to the approach and implementation of treatment for juvenile delinquents.
> 2. I want to become more knowledgeable of the actual offenses committed by the offenders and the possible consequences that follow them.
> 3. I would like to understand the overall functioning of the juvenile justice system in more detail.
> 4. Through interaction with the youth, I aspire to see if I am able to establish a balance with them, similar to the relationship that exists between a therapist and client.
> 5. I want to apply theories of juvenile delinquency that I have learned in the classroom, to actual practice within the context of the agency.
>
> After the establishment of my goals, I determined the following objectives to achieve my goals and to evaluate my progress:
>
> 1. I will review my course materials on sociological and criminological theories regarding juvenile delinquency.
> 2. I will plan appointments and discuss with the Psych-Solutions' therapist the techniques they use to both reach and treat the juveniles.
> 3. I will perform a thorough review of juvenile case files to achieve a better understanding of the criminal offenses and court system.
> 4. I will conduct detailed interviews with the juveniles to gain a better understanding into the lives of the youths.

5. I will play the role of mentor in and outside the classroom to develop rapport with them.
6. I will keep a detailed record of my emotions and experiences I am exposed to throughout my internship.
7. I will confer with my agency supervisor on her perceived view of my skills and completion of assignments.

First and foremost, I learned that the most powerful outside source affecting the operation of this facility is politics/bureaucracy. Politics not only has a huge influence upon the budget, it also affects the hiring, discretion, and admission of particular offenders. For example, I offer the case of "Jimmy." (The name has been changed for the purpose of confidentiality).

Jimmy has been noted for displaying the beginning signs of psychoses/schizophrenia, but cannot be officially diagnosed as schizophrenic until he is 18. He laughs spontaneously, not only at himself, but also at inanimate objects. Jimmy talks to such objects as the wall and bath towel. He rarely verbally responds to any questions that are directed to him. However, when he does talk, his speech is very slow, delayed, and drawn out. According to the superintendent and therapist, the MHH is not a proper placement for Jimmy. His psychiatric treatment needs are beyond the scope of those offered through this program. However, according to the legislature, since the MHH has a mental health component, it has to serve him. When thousands of dollars are allocated to this facility for its multi-trained therapists, the legislature cannot understand why Jimmy cannot be treated there. The legislative body does not see the actual child's behavior and the extensive help he needs, only the money being provided for mental health services. Therefore, this child will probably slip through the cracks of the system.

Another political issue is that due to the increase in juvenile crime and a larger number of youths being direct filed, the treatment component of moderate risk programs is being de-emphasized and is being replaced with a more prison-like environment. This happened to MHH, during the middle of my internship when a new superintendent was brought in to make the transition.

. . . [A]fter interviewing several of the clients and staff, I was able to draw conclusions as to the overall opinion of the most important issues and practices confronting them. It was the general consensus that the largest problem was the lack of consistency in the behavior modification system.

The following views of a youth and a teacher offer intuitive insight into program and creative ideas for consideration for its improvement.

Interview with Juvenile #1

Question (Q) *How have you benefited from this program? What can you take from here to apply to your life in a positive way?*

Response (R) I have become more respectful toward authority and also more able to get into a routine for my life. All of these things that I have learned have helped me even more to becoming a paramedic.

Q *What do you like about this program?*

R I like the encouragement from selected staff that I am going to make it somewhere.

Q *What would you change about this program?*

R I would get rid of group accountability, have more staff on the floor, more hands-on treatment, more consistent reward and punishment system, and more benefits for the managers.

Q *What do you plan to do with your life upon release?*

R I plan to go to work with my mom in the Everglades.

Q *How do you think the arrival of the new superintendent has affected the program?*

R This program is supposed to be a halfway house, and he is taking away all of our personal hygiene items. He is making this a more high-risk facility program when the boys are not high risk. It is a Level 6 program.

Q *What aspect of the program has helped you the most?*

R Family sessions because things are discussed that were never talked about before. Also, group sessions are helpful because they give me more knowledge of topics discussed, such as: stress, anger, victim awareness, and substance abuse.

Interview with Teacher #1

Q *How do you feel the arrival of the new superintendent has affected the program?*

R Positively, with a lot of hope and expectations because of the new ideas that are being brought in. The negative points of the change in administration are that there are too many changes too rapidly without a clear substitution of methods and techniques to maintain order and proper facility management.

Q *What aspects of the program at MHH would you change?*

R I would provide a consequence-free channel for the clients to express their concerns, frustrations, and needs with the expectancy that something positive will result.

Q *What are the strengths and weakness of this program?*

R Strengths: Overall, personnel commitment to the welfare of the offenders is high. Also, the concern for increased structure and quality of care is a positive as well. Weakness: Inconsistencies in maintaining proper structure and administration of consequences.

Q *What techniques do you use to leave an impact on the boys?*

R My techniques are to be a positive role model by the actions of my life, rather than words.

Q *How do you think your unique role plays into the treatment of the offenders?*

R I attempt to be consistently fair and nonjudgmental about the many issues and challenge that confront me on a daily basis.

Q *What are your expectations/goals for the youths?*

R My expectations are that maybe something that they hear or see from me will allow them to make a better decision in the educational and personal challenges that are waiting just around the corner for them.

Q *Do you feel that the program successfully treats/rehabilitates the offenders?*

R Yes, because the facility attends to their root causes as to why they are here. The juvenile justice system at large does not because the youth are sent back the same environment and social structure that got them here, without any attempt to correct the malignancies that have perpetuated from one generation to another. For the six to nine months that the youth are here, they get better food, care, more attention to their individual needs than ever before, and more structure is implemented. However, all that is corroded when they are put back in the old circumstances.

Q *What improvements would you suggest for the juvenile justice system?*

R I would address the home environment with equal or greater tenacity than is currently enforced on youth for their crimes.

Whereas my agency supervisor was helpful in directing me to staff members and clients who were willing to be interviewed, she was not as helpful in setting my performance standards and expectations that I should uphold in this program. Her expectations of me were not clearly defined and became more confusing with the change of the administrator. Nonetheless, I did obtain skills and realized certain strengths that I never would have realized I possessed if it was not for the administrator change and a longstanding situation I was confronted with. The lack of clear and detailed expectations to what I should have been aware of in my role of intern caused an insufficient path of communication between my supervisor and myself. I had chosen this particular agency because of the opportunity that it afforded me to working hands-on with juvenile delinquents. (My primary assignment was to handle all medical-related duties.) I would complete these tasks as quickly as possible to observe the counseling sessions. My supervisor, however, misinterpreted my intentions as only being concerned with the boys and to be blowing off my assignments. To continue being an asset both to the clients and to the agency, this situation forced me to reevaluate my work ethic and performance and direct them toward my supervisor's value system, not my own. After this problem was identified in my mid-term evaluation and discussed with my internship supervisor, I made sure that the moment I walked in the door, I glowed with motivation and spirit, ready to take on any task that was asked of me and perform it above and beyond the satisfaction level of my agency supervisor. My renegotiated plan led not only to taking my experience in a more positive direction, but also to my agency supervisor giving me an excellent rating on my final evaluation. I turned what at times was a very stressful, uncomfortable situation into something that increased my personal growth and individual development in a positive direction. I learned how to deal appropriately with difficult situations and developed coping skills in dealing with problems faced in the workplace and in working closely with someone of a different value system.

... Overall, I greatly enjoyed my experience as an intern at the MHH. The one-on-one time I was able to have with the juveniles was invaluable to my future career as a forensic psychologist (Magyar, 2003, pp. 3–13).

This reflective statement from another intern at the MHH illustrates a problem that was encountered and resolved midway through the internship.

... In the *Sociology/Criminology Internship Placement Pamphlet*, it stated, "the purpose of the internship program is to provide 'hands on' experience in a criminal justice agency" (University of Miami, 2003, p. 3). Because I have computer and office experience, I was asked on numerous occasions to stay in the Social Services office and retype policies. Initially, I did not mind doing this because I wanted to help the MHH be better prepared for their next Inspector General Inspection. But when I was doing this work for 39 of the first 42 hours I was interning, I told my supervisor. She assured me things would change and that I would get less paperwork and more hands-on experience with the offenders.

This transition did not go well with those who repeatedly asked me to type their work. One staff member told me in a harsh tone, "These policies are more important than your attending Level Review." I told the staff member, "It's more important to you, but not to my internship experience," and went to Level Review (Lozada, 2003, p. 15).

This scenario is an excellent example of what is unacceptable during the internship process. It is imperative for interns to contact their agency supervisors whenever staff members attempt to intimidate them to do their work.

Consider the following student's observation and problems encountered while interning at the Office of the State Attorney.

This experience has brought me many new perspectives of the external world. In my first day of internship, the agency supervisor gave me a 20-page long "Intern Handbook." It was surprising to me when she told me that I would not be allowed to be a bartender when I am interning; also, I am not allowed to work as a volunteer in some nonprofit agencies—for example, agencies that deal with victims or witnesses. The purpose is to avoid conflict of interest and to avoid contact with people who may influence judicial decisions, since I may release confidential information to them that may alter their decision/testimonies.

The main problem I encountered was feeling caught in the middle of bad communication between my assigned attorney and her supervisor.

In each general unit of the Office of the State Attorney there are three assistant attorneys (ASAs), a Division Chief attorney (DC) [the supervising attorney]; and "A," "B," and "C" prosecutors (the "pit" assistants). The "C" prosecutor handles new incoming felony cases. With more experience, the ASA is promoted to a "B" and then an "A" prosecutor. I work with a "C" ASA, Maggie. Although in theory, she has the "easiest" cases because of her light experience, her workload is unbelievable. She handles more than 120 cases at a time. Her cases include burglary, DUI, traffic offenses, aggravated assaults, and probation violations. Her duty is to articulate the progress of these cases, including a great deal of paperwork and numerous phone calls. Although she has assistants—a victim-witness coordinator, a secretary, and an intern (at this time)—she often works overtime and during the weekends.

From my point of view, Maggie is a very responsible, hard-working, and easy going ASA. Unfortunately, she has problems with her supervisor, the DC in the general unit, and the secretary. It seems that the DC has disliked Maggie since she arrived in the office. He has not offered her much help in sentencing guidelines and the operation of the system as other DCs. Once I observed the two having a verbal dispute over a small matter. . . . Maggie forgot to complete a task her DC asked her to do earlier. Two days later she received an e-mail from the State Attorney inviting her to a conference over a matter of a "discriminative" nature. The DC had filed a complaint stating that Maggie had been disrespectful to him. After the meeting, Maggie received probation and a warning, which may affect her promotion prospects. I felt Maggie did not deserve this because I witnessed a very minor dispute. When I questioned her about the situation, she stated that her supervisor had more "weight" in the office than she did. It appeared to me that instead of going through a thorough investigation (which would include interviewing those present) before deciding a resolution, the system made a hasty decision in order to protect the hierarchy of authority. After the incident, I realized that it is easy for people with authority to manipulate their power against people in subordinate positions.

Not only did I observe Maggie's problems with the secretary, but I was also personally drawn into them. For some reasons, court files and incoming documents that come through the secretary would be lost. On some occasions, when Maggie asked the secretary to send legal documents, she never sent them. Eventually Maggie received complaints from defense attorneys, victims, or officers. Because of these incidents, Maggie lost confidence in the secretary and asked me to take up some of her duties. Despite the heavier workload, I was glad to take up some of the work because it provided learning opportunities. Albeit, I always attempted to keep my natural position of an observer/outsider in their obscure conflict, I had difficulty relating to the secretary because of her insolence. She often talks on personal calls, leaves the office early, and does many other things that she should not be doing as a secretary. Furthermore, her insolence becomes an obstacle in the process of the division of labor.

As the obscure conflict continued overtime, I had a dilemma about whom I should trust. Maggie would complain to me about the secretary; on the other hand, the secretary would call me while Maggie was not in her office, pretending to look for her, but her true intention was to tell me that Maggie had left some file somewhere—which implied that Maggie was a careless person and responsible for the lost files. Because I didn't want to be in the middle of this dispute, I reported verbally the content of the calls to Maggie each time the secretary called me. It was obvious to me that the secretary wanted me as an ally to exaggerate the problem and cause Maggie additional problems with her DC. Unfortunately, she underestimated my intelligence and the communication between Maggie and me. I became more comfortable with this situation after I attended the second seminar given by the university's supervisor, at which time she reminded us that if we encountered any problem in the placement, we should contact her immediately. I did and received the necessary advice to handle the uncomfortable situation and received the full benefit of my internship (Lam, 2003, pp. 3–8).

One student interning at JRE Lee Alternative School shares his disenchantment with his choice of interaction for accomplishing his goals while working with the students and the insight into his own personal growth.

My role at JRE Lee was a mentor/counselor; it was my responsibility to positively stimulate students. I arrived the first day of school not knowing what to expect. As an intern, I was obviously an outsider for two reasons: my conservative attire and my fresh face. I was unsure how students would respond to my visibly alien features. However, it did not take long to find an effective approach to earn their trust. The student who compared the school environment to *Blood In, Blood Out* provided the answer. Because I had recently seen the movie, my response sparked both a conversation and the student's interest in me. My approach then was to interact with students on their level, to find common ground, and to relate what interests them to my counseling sessions. It provided motivation and allowed them to open up. However, such an approach had its limitations because I traded authoritative respect for trust. I became a friend to my specific students, which manifested itself in their desire to eat lunch with me or defend my presence to other students, but I was not perceived as an authoritative figure; students never followed my instructions or commands since I was treated as one of them. I realized that my approach was ineffective; I found it difficult to inspire them.

My own views stemming either from my life experiences or from classroom materials could have been a valuable resource for students in developing or reexamining their own views about self, world, and others. However, just as the dispositions of the students prevented the teachers from doing their job, so too did they for me. During one-on-one sessions, I believed my students recognized the value of my advice, yet their desire to save face superseded any desire to change. Respect appeared to be at the apex of their value system. Their irrational and disruptive behavior, although learned, functioned as a defense or protective mechanism to maintain that respect. It was very frustrating for me to witness a seeming internalization of my advice, but as soon as my students were free from supervision, to witness a total disregard for it. I came to understand, though, how important respect was in terms of survival, both within this school and within subcultures.

One benefit of my internship related to my own self-improvement. Knowledge gained from new experiences provided the potential or an assessment of my life up until this point and for the incorporation of different life perspectives into my own. Everyone, including myself, sees the world through his or her own filers or schemas. This internship experience was very humbling. It allowed me to not only reconsider how fortunate I am coming from a middle-class background, but to also expunge much of the ignorance that has influenced my view of the world. The frequent interactions with students challenged many of the stereotypes that I blindly followed and that dictated my evaluation of certain people. They caused me to question many things, specifically the sources of many maladaptive behaviors and the extent to which students alone were responsible for them. Granted, it was a matter of choice to attend school and get an education, but various life circumstances blinded these students to options available to them as well as an awareness of their potential benefits.

Gradually, I became aware of these problems as my internship progressed and my recognition of them influenced my decision to set specific goals in addition to those customary for the internship. I chose to use the wisdom and values I have gained throughout my life toward the redirection of principles certain students hold, to provide a different but valuable perspective on life, and if compelled, to reevaluate my ideals and thus cultivate my present value system. I had hoped the counseling would have stimulated my students to aspire, but their desire for respect permeated throughout and distorted their entire value system. I rarely observed any development in my students and my continual discontent shaped my current decision not to follow a similar career path (Hellebrand, 2003, pp. 13–16).

Most of the interns in our program have treated the agency supervisors with much respect and professionalism. There is one placement, however, that I will always remember as a student's internship supervisor's nightmare. For the purpose of confidentiality we will call the student Ms. B.

After one week at her placement Ms. B. came to me and explained that she was extremely uncomfortable in the juvenile detention center. After a lengthy discussion, I agreed to place her in the juvenile alternative sanctions system (a less threatening environment). Two weeks later her supervisor called to inform me of a confrontation between them, wherein Ms. B. used profanity, and made the decision to terminate her placement. I contacted Ms. B. and was informed (with the use of profanity) that "they just don't like me and they don't want me there." After a brief period Ms. B. became calm and agreed to return and apologize to her supervisor. I called her supervisor and informed her that Ms. B. would be returning and apologizing. The next day I received a fax stating the following:

> Dr. Taylor:
>
> As agreed, we are faxing you documentation and evaluation of Ms. B. Ms. B. did not call yesterday as specifically instructed to do so by you. Therefore, we have no choice but to terminate her. This morning at 8:40 A.M. Ms. Nichols had a call/message from her. Ms. B. stated that everything was OK and she would not be in today because she has a doctor's appointment, but she would be in tomorrow. As of now, we still consider Ms. B. terminated and will *consider* reinstating her if she does *all* of the following:
>
> 1. Apologizes to all parties concerned.
> 2. Meets with supervisory staff to discuss her overall unsatisfactory job performance.
> 3. Adheres to guidelines, directives, and corrective action plan developed by supervisory staff.
>
> We will keep you abreast of new developments as they arise.

The short version of the conclusion is that Ms. B. returned to the agency for one week and, according to the supervisor, she "became arrogant, defensive, confrontive, disrespectful, and rude and left. She did not complete her 240 hours. She could not be contacted by telephone and did not return to my office."

The following is an incident report that was submitted to an agency supervisor regarding an internship nightmare experienced by one of our students (Ms. G).

> Subject: Incident Involving Lt. C and Det. M
>
> I request that you look into the situation reported below, since it could affect my status as an intern and/or my future in a law enforcement career.
>
> On June 26, 1997, at approximately 8:00 P.M., while riding with the Street Narcotics Unit (SNU), an unrelated incident took place in the area in which the SNU was operating. I remained with Officer M while other officers from the SNU proceeded to the area of the second incident. I learned eventually that the second incident had to do with a police shooting.
>
> In the early morning hours of June 27, 1997, I received a call from Sergeant N of the Homicide Unit. I was told to come immediately to the central station to have my statement taken regarding what I had witnessed. I proceeded to the station, where I arrived at 6:00 A.M. I was held there until 10:30 A.M., even after I had stated several times that I had to go to work. I was questioned by Lt. C, Sgt. N, and Det. M regarding the incident and I replied truthfully and to the best of my knowledge to their questions. They insinuated that I was covering something up and that I was not being totally honest in my answers, even to the

extent that they submitted me to a voice stress analyzer. As a result of the test, Det. M told me I was being deceptive. I informed him I was telling them what I best recollected from the previous evening.

On July 2, 1997 I was called by Lt. C, who asked me to come to the station once again. I was questioned about my previous answers. I was told by Lt. C and Det. M that I had not been truthful. Lt. C told me that he did not want to see me "get myself in trouble for hiding something"; he also stated that I was "jeopardizing my career in this field and my life." Due to what I perceived as threats and Det. M's yelling at me, I claimed that I was not a criminal and should not be treated as such. Det. M indicated that "the jails are full of innocent people." I responded to both Lt. C and Det. M that I had been truthful in my previous responses, and that I should not be treated as a common criminal. The detective indicated that I was there on the scene as an observer and that my job was to observe, and "I had not observed s---."

I feel that I have been treated unfairly in this matter. I have cooperated fully and truthfully, yet I am viewed differently by those conducting the inquiry in the above-mentioned matter. I have spoken to my internship coordinator at the university and have been advised to discontinue my riding assignments until she speaks with you and clarifies the situation.

The student was not required to return to this field placement, but did complete her hours at another site. She was, however, summoned to appear at the trial of the accused officer, but was not called to testify. She was ordered to appear at an upcoming trial three years later (2000) for another officer allegedly involved in the incident, after which her nightmare finally ended.

SUMMARY

In your internship, you may think that you are filling two roles: as a student and as an employee. It is important for you to remember, however, that you are primarily a student in the role of a participant observer and secondarily, an employee. As a participant-observer, your objectives are to absorb all you can about your agency as it applies to your desired goal of entering the field of criminal justice-criminology and recording staff interactions and agency events and situations objectively.

Once you determine what is important for you to observe, you need to decide the method you want to use to record your observations. In this chapter it is recommended that you keep a journal for recording your daily experiences. Some supervisors suggest the use of a diary (similar to a journal), which is set up like a calendar but includes no systematic way of recording data, whereas others suggest the use of log-books or field notebooks. Whatever method you use, you must remember to maintain confidentiality whenever you write or discuss your entries.

The most popular interviewing method is the personal interview, which may be conducted with or without a tape recorder. If you choose to audiotape the interviews, it is necessary to get permission from the interviewees before you do so.

Prior to the interviews, you should also have a good notion of the areas or subjects on which you will focus in collecting and recording the desired information.

Preparing an interview guide can contribute to successful interviews with a few staff members who have specific knowledge of your area of interest. For the purpose of organization, the guide should include a face sheet that covers the social characteristics of the interviewees. When confidentiality is an issue, use a code number instead of a name on the face sheet.

As an intern, the most important thing to remember is to do your best. This does not necessarily mean that you must be everything to everybody. It is important to set high standards for yourself but to understand the difference between high standards and unreasonable expectations. Above all, keep in mind that your primary goal is to learn, not to demonstrate what you know. You should expect the agency staff to be more educated and experienced than you, but you should not allow their training to intimidate you. Their expertise is what you are counting on to provide you with one of the most exciting educational experiences of your life. Relax, go for it, and take advantage of this great opportunity.

DISCUSSION QUESTIONS

1. How should a student orient him- or herself with the internship? What is the most effective way to begin any internship in which the staff and clients do not know you?
2. What are the various methods of data collection?
3. What factors should be considered upon setting up a student in an appropriate internship? What are the consequences of not accomplishing this careful and necessary process?
4. How can students benefit from peers experiencing similar internships?

CHAPTER

6

Supervision

QUESTIONS FOR STUDENTS

Who will provide supervision during your internship?

What type of relationship will you have with your supervisor?

Why do you need to understand the supervisory process?

THE AGENCY'S PERSPECTIVE

From the agency's perspective, internship programs provide a valuable pool of job applicants. Since most internships in the criminal justice system do not pay stipends, some interns have stated that agencies consider internships a source of cheap labor (Khoury, 1993). Although some agencies use interns to perform menial tasks, such as running errands or performing secretarial tasks, including filing, photocopying, and typing, most agencies consider internship programs a tremendous benefit to them. As one agency executive put it: "There are reams of hard and soft benefits that make intern programs an invaluable recruitment tool" (quoted in Scott, 1992, p. 60).

Several of my students have been hired by the Office of the State Attorney, the Department of Corrections, and various other criminal justice agencies after they completed their internships. Their agency supervisors have told me that interns who are reliable, hardworking, and personable and who demonstrate the skills necessary to perform the tasks required for available positions are the first to be considered for job openings because their agency supervisors have firsthand knowledge of their character and ability. In any case, interns will become recruiters for these agencies by encouraging other students on campus to apply for these internship placements. This process fits with the goals of agencies whose primary way of filling entry-level positions is by recruiting recent college graduates (Scott, 1992, p. 62).

Internship programs are also cost effective because agencies do not have to allocate funds for campus-recruitment programs if their interns are doing the recruiting. According to Chastain (1990, p. 180), a good program uses the interns' time to "produce as useful an output as possible [and] that causes the intern to want to seek post-graduation employment in the company."

The Internet has become a very useful resource in providing web-based support for gathering information on internship placements. Several colleges and universities use their web servers to promote their internship programs.

DEFINING FIELD SUPERVISION

The first considerations for many students in choosing an internship placement are the clients (adults or juveniles), location of the agency and concerns about transportation, and hours of operation (whether the agency is open in the evenings and on weekends). Although these are important concerns, it has been my experience that supervision by and interaction with the professionals with whom you will work is the most important factor to be considered.

During your internship experience, you will be under the supervision of a faculty member from your college or university (the internship coordinator) and a staff member at the placement site (the agency supervisor). As discussed at greater length later in the chapter, the internship coordinator observes your progress and interfaces with your agency supervisor and other appropriate staff members at the internship site.

In your fieldwork you will work closely with your agency supervisor while reporting regularly to your internship coordinator. They are both responsible for monitoring the performance of your daily assignments and should be kept completely informed of your activities and notified immediately of any difficulties or problems you may have that would impede your individual and professional growth.

Therefore, the basic question you must ask yourself about a supervisor is whether you can work with this person and if he or she is interested in helping you learn. For many internship placements, the internship coordinators have made previous site visits and are acquainted with the agency supervisors and their qualifications. For those of you who must find your own placements, it is important to consider the supervisor's personality, qualifications, areas of interest, and desire and ability to provide adequate time for supervision and training. It is also important to know whether you need a more nurturing environment in which the supervisor provides a great deal of direction (the agency-centered model of supervision) or less direction and greater autonomy (the student-centered model of supervision). In summary, you should select a supervisor with the ability and willingness to work with you to meet best your personal and educational needs.

Most agencies use a student-centered model of supervision, whereby students must arrange their interactions with the internship coordinator, the agency supervisor, and their peers and determine the amount of supervisory interaction they want to have (Gordon and McBride, 1990, p. 48). The agency-centered model of supervision is being used more and more frequently (see Figure 6.1). In this model, interns' interactions are coordinated by the chief executive officers (president and vice president) of the organization.

It is not unusual for students initially to feel dependent on their supervisors. For example, one of my students reported that her first day in a prison internship

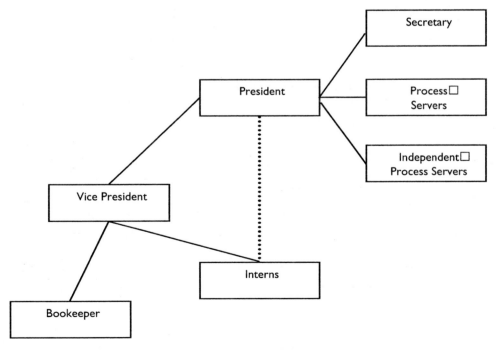

Figure 6.1   Sample Informal Agency Structure: Agency-Centered Model of Supervision—Organizational Breakdown

was strange. Her supervisor had to attend a meeting and left her with other staff members who "did not know what to do" with her. During the course of your internship, your relationship with your supervisor will become less dependent and more reciprocal with an exchange of the supervisor's feedback and your input.

ROLE OF THE AGENCY SUPERVISOR

The agency supervisor plays a crucial role in guiding a student's training experiences and in most cases will long be remembered as a key motivator. Located at the site, the supervisor can provide educational opportunities that are impossible to obtain in the classroom. In a successful placement, the supervisor will become a supportive and skilled mentor whom you will view as a role model for your future professional life. Unfortunately, this has not been the case for some interns who have found the relationships with their supervisors to be inadequate and demeaning. In such a case, your only recourse is to report any incidents to your internship coordinator, since the evaluation of supervisors is often a sensitive issue in an agency and rarely covers work with interns (Norcross, Strausser, and Faltus, 1988).

The best ways to get to know potential supervisors is to have personal meetings or phone interview with them. It is my practice to have interns phone and schedule personal interviews. Along with other pertinent information, such as your academic training and practical experiences, mentioned in Chapter 3, the supervisor will be interested in your personality, reliability, work ethic, and how well you follow instructions. These factors will assist the supervisor in assessing if it will be worth the time to supervise you.

Once you and your internship coordinator know that a particular supervisor can devote sufficient time to your learning experience, you should make arrangements to sign an internship agreement that specifies the terms of the internship and type of work you will perform. See Figure 6.2 for a sample of the internship agreement used in my course. Along with this agreement, you should be given information on your routine, hours, the agency's rules and regulations, and schedule for supervision.

Your agency supervisor should inform you of the appropriate codes of dress and conduct as well. He or she should determine the availability and appropriateness of supplemental reading material and make a general timetable for orientation and ongoing fieldwork activities. It is desirable for your agency supervisor to provide purposeful contact with the realities of the agency's day-to-day work. He or she should make sure that your work assignments throughout the term depend on your learning needs and abilities, keeping in mind that your work should be of value to the agency but that you should not have the same workload as a regular employee. Because it is not always possible to work with your agency supervisor

Name of Intern _____

Dear Intern Supervisor:

To provide our interns with the best possible learning experience, we ask that you consider the following agreement between the Department of Sociology Internship Office and your agency.

The agency agrees to:

...provide meaningful criminal justice related activity to the student. Clerical work, filing, phone answering, etc. will be kept at a minimum;

...contact the Internship Coordinator if any questions or problems arise with the student or the program itself;

...the best of its ability, not to put the student in a life-threatening situation;

...not use the student in an undercover capacity;

...monitor the student's hours and make sure he/she puts in the required 240 hours during the semester;

...evaluate each intern twice during the semester.

The Intern Supervisor will be responsible for addressing safety issues, policy and procedures, and other relevant information, with each intern.

The Intern Supervisor agrees that the Internship Coordinator may visit during the semester to meet with the supervisor and the student.

We look forward to an exciting year for our interns and thank you for your participation in our program.

_____	Date	_____	Date
Department of Sociology Internship Coordinator		Internship Supervisor	
		_____	
		Position	
		_____	
		Agency	

Figure 6.2 Sample Internship Agency Agreement

on a daily basis, you and your supervisor should arrange regular sessions to discuss weekly events, goals that have been accomplished, future goals, and the status of your professional development. In short, your relationship with the agency supervisor serves as the medium through which you can make maximum use of the knowledge you bring to the placement and can help to develop your skills and accept new concepts and ideas.

ROLE OF THE FACULTY SUPERVISOR

Interns are supervised by a faculty supervisor and an agency supervisor. This section focuses on the faculty supervisor. This type of supervision differs from agency supervision, in which there is constant monitoring of a student's performance. The amount of faculty supervision a student receives will depend largely on the person's need to pursue it in meeting a goal of enhancing personal and professional development. This should be a mutual relationship, with the students giving input and the faculty supervisor providing constructive feedback. The relationship should move from dependence to interdependence to independence. This relationship will move through these steps more easily if both participants are able to express fears. My students have shared their fears of not being able to perform required tasks well enough to receive satisfactory evaluations and of appearing "stupid;" I have shared my fears with them of interns' doing something that will jeopardize themselves or the agency placement for future interns. Because faculty supervisors are ultimately accountable for ensuring that interns meet professional and educational standards, they are extremely concerned about the interns' attitudes toward performing high-quality work at the agencies, as well as the interns' academic performance. Therefore, the primary responsibility of faculty supervisors is to ensure that all interns are prepared and apply themselves diligently and responsibly to fulfill their obligations to the agencies and the university.

Although the university and the agency accept shared accountability for designing useful assignments and other educational events to fulfill the instructional goals of the internship program, the faculty supervisor shoulders the primary responsibility for administering and managing field education and acts as a liaison between the school and the agency. The faculty supervisor will determine the course requirements, direct a student's internship education, and enter into an agreement with the agency supervisor that the student will be given the opportunity to observe and participate in various agency assignments.

ADMINISTRATIVE AND MANAGEMENT RESPONSIBILITIES

The internship coordinator provides leadership in

1. Developing and monitoring placements
2. Placing and replacing students
3. Devising methods of obtaining necessary information for making placements
4. Determining the criteria for the internship course
5. Developing and implementing policies and procedures related to fieldwork

6. Designating field (agency) supervisors
7. Representing the university in relationships with agencies

To determine the most suitable field placement for a student, the faculty supervisor meets with the student to discuss the student's concerns and professional aspirations. At this time, the faculty supervisor asks the student to fill out various forms to provide additional information necessary for establishing a proper field placement and gives the student a copy of the syllabus. (See Figure 6.3 for a sample syllabus.)

After the student is placed in an agency, the faculty supervisor monitors the student's performance, and if deemed unsuitable (a rare occurrence), the faculty supervisor arranges for the student to be placed in a more appropriate agency. This decision should be made early enough in the process so that the student has the opportunity to fulfill the requirements of the second placement.

Term Paper: _____

DUE DATE:

INTERNSHIP GRADE
The following will determine your final grade:
1. agency supervisor's (midterm) evaluation
2. agency supervisor's (final) evaluation
3. internship (term) paper

TEXTBOOK
Taylor, Dorothy L., *Jumpstarting Your Career: An Internship Guide for Criminal Justice,* Prentice Hall, 2004. It is suggested that you read the entire text. However, Chapters 1 through 5 are required. Chapters 1 through 3 should be read before you begin your internship; they will be helpful in establishing your goals and objectives for this course. Chapters 4 and 5 will be useful for the term paper.

SUPERVISOR EVALUATIONS
The agency supervisor will evaluate your performance twice during the semester. The first evaluation serves primarily to indicate any problem areas (see the sample evaluation form).
The faculty supervisor will discuss these evaluations with you. **IT IS YOUR RESPONSIBILITY TO MAKE SURE THESE EVALUATIONS ARE COMPLETED AND SUBMITTED.**

INTERNSHIP TERM PAPER
You will submit a *detailed* outline before you to submit the final paper.
Present the term paper in an observation/participation style. Compare what you observed and experienced in the real world or at your agency with the criminological concepts and issues you learned in the classroom (see the sample outline in Figure 6.4).
The term paper should be typed double spaced. It should also be free of spelling and grammatical errors and should include a bibliography, with all sources properly cited. The paper should be at least 15 pages.

Figure 6.3   Sample Syllabus

If a student finds his or her own placement (for example, one that is closer to home during the summer when he or she is not taking other classes on campus), the faculty supervisor first determines that the student's work will be of value to the particular agency. Then he or she contacts the agency the student has suggested, establishes a relationship with the agency supervisor, and makes sure that the agency will provide the appropriate experience for the student.

ADVISEMENT AND LIAISON ACTIVITIES

Along with academic advisement, the faculty supervisor provides support to the student when emotional or interpersonal difficulties occur during the field placement. As was stated earlier, it is helpful for faculty supervisors and interns to relate honestly at the beginning of their relationship about their shared and individual needs and concerns. This will eliminate much anxiety, ineffective communication, and frustration. Baird's (1996, p. 58) list of supervisors' and interns' needs to be considered is helpful:

- *Supervisors' needs:* honesty and integrity, ethical conduct, openness to suggestion, respect for the supervisor's experience, careful work of high quality, deep thought, hard work, and willingness to listen even if there is disagreement
- *Interns' needs:* support, patience, knowledge of the field, guidance, accessibility, modeling, direct teaching of information, involvement, some autonomy, trust, openness, and willingness to listen

To prevent interns from making mistakes and to help them achieve the most beneficial learning experience, it is crucial for the faculty supervisor to explain his or her requirements to interns at the onset of their internships. The interns should know the frequency and time of supervisory meetings, the content of the meetings (for example, for group discussions or individual journal reviews), and whether both personal and professional issues will be dealt with.

Some faculty supervisors make a minimum of three site visits per academic semester: (1) before the student is placed (in some cases during the preceding semester), (2) during the week of midterm examinations, and (3) before the week of final examinations. Additional visits are made, when necessary, to support the student's instructional agenda. The faculty supervisor also maintains regular telephone contact with the student (as well as with first-time agency supervisors), especially during the initial phase of placement, to resolve problems immediately. Although inappropriate placements are rare, early visits and telephone calls by your faculty supervisor to the agency can determine that you have been inappropriately placed to obtain the desired internship experience. For example, one site visit and two follow-up telephone calls determined that one of our interns, who was placed in a residential treatment program for delinquent adolescent girls expecting to have one-on-one contact by tutoring the girls, was working on the switchboard most of the time. This student was reassigned to another agency, where she experienced a more fulfilling internship.

ACADEMIC ASSIGNMENTS

Your faculty supervisor will influence your internship education significantly through assigned readings, journal reports, observations of various features of the agency environment, and term papers. Your journal reports and other written communications will assist your faculty supervisor in overseeing your progress and enable him or her to help you solve any problems or strengthen any weaknesses that may be interfering with your personal and professional growth. It is natural to want to avoid discussing your weaknesses or concerns for fear of receiving an unsatisfactory grade, but if you are not meeting the agency's requirements, you will almost guarantee an unsatisfactory grade. Your faculty supervisor anticipates that some problems may occur and that you may experience some anxieties regarding your performance during your introductory experience with criminal justice professionals.

During the internship experience, students assume the role of participant-observers. They investigate the setting, the role of the various staff members, individuals, and the activity of the agency. In periodic seminars (at least three per semester), they present ongoing situations from their current work in their field agencies to their faculty supervisor and fellow internship students, and during finals week, they submit a direct-observation term paper of their internship experience. (For a sample outline for a term paper, see Figure 6.4 .)

EVALUATION AND GRADING

The faculty supervisor is responsible for assigning the final letter grade in fieldwork, in consultation with the agency supervisor, at the end of the semester in which the student interned. It should be noted, however, that the evaluation of students is an ongoing process and that each seminar is considered a period of evaluation. The faculty supervisor is at a disadvantage in that he or she cannot directly observe the interns' performance at the fieldwork sites. Other than sporadic visits to the agencies and occasional telephone conferences with the agency supervisors, the faculty supervisor must rely on the agency supervisors' views of students' accomplishments in the field. Therefore, the faculty supervisor grades students on the basis of the agency supervisors' two field evaluations (see Figure 6.5 for a sample evaluation form) and the students' achievement of goals, participation in seminar, field notes, and term papers. The weight of each of these elements in determining the students' final grades differs, depending on the grading system used by a particular faculty supervisor.

I. INTRODUCTION
   A. *Brief* overview of the agency, including:
      1. Type of agency (local, state, federal, law enforcement, court, corrections, and so forth)
      2. Size
      3. History
   B. Organizational structure (including your location in that structure)
      1. Goals
      2. Objectives

II. REVIEW OF THE CRIMINOLOGY LITERATURE
   A. A discussion of issues, problems, and practices relevant to the agency (such as budget con-straints, legal changes, increasing crime rates, effects of prison over-crowding, effects of increasing public attitudes toward getting tough on crime)
   B. How does the literature address these issues?
   C. Refer to both published articles and books and course work materials (textbook or class notes)

III. PLACEMENT AGENCY: OBSERVATIONS AND FINDINGS
   A. What actually happens in the agency?
      1. What do you do?
      2. According to the agency, what issues, problems, and practices are most important?
   B. Review selected agency documents
      1. Is the agency fulfilling its mission?

IV. SUMMARY AND DISCUSSION
   A. Synthesize your agency placement experience and themes from the criminology literature and course materials.
   B. How has your criminological understanding been enhanced or changed by this experience?
      1. What ideas have helped you understand your experience?
      2. What works? What does not?

V. BIBLIOGRAPHY: See any criminal justice/criminology textbook for the proper format.

Figure 6.4   Sample Outline for Term Paper

ADVOCACY AND GRIEVANCE PROCEDURES

If you have a grievance with your agency supervisor, discuss it with the supervisor. However, there are exceptions. You may encounter some problems that should be discussed with your faculty supervisor before you confront your agency supervisor. These problems may be ethical (accepting free food while on ride-alongs with police officers) or methodological (observing a difference from theory to practice, such as violations of *Miranda* rights). If you and your agency supervisor cannot resolve your difficulties, you should confer with the faculty supervisor or with another faculty member, the department chairperson, or the dean. When there is a controversy regarding grades, you should comply with the university's policy on reassessing grades.

Student's Name   _____
Social Security No.   _____
Agency   _____
Intern's Agency
Supervisor   _____
Position   _____
Address of Agency   _____
Phone No. of Agency   _____

YOUR COOPERATION IN MAKING THIS INTERNSHIP AVAILABLE TO OUR STUDENTS IS
GREATLY APPRECIATED. AS THE INTERNSHIP DRAWS TO A CLOSE, IT WOULD BE MOST HELP-
FUL TO ME IF YOU WOULD COMPLETE THIS EVALUATION FORM AND RETURN YOUR COM-
MENTS TO ME IN THE SELF-ADDRESSED ENVELOPE THAT IS ENCLOSED.

THIS EVALUATION IS AN EXTREMELY IMPORTANT TOOL IN PROVIDING INFORMATION
PARAMOUNT TO THE STUDENT'S ACADEMIC AND PROFESSIONAL DEVELOPMENT. I WILL
REVIEW THE EVALUATION WITH THE STUDENT. A COPY OF THE EVALUATION WILL BE
PLACED IN THE STUDENT'S FILE.

IF YOU THINK THAT FURTHER COMMENTS ARE NECESSARY, FEEL FREE TO PROVIDE ADDI-
TIONAL INFORMATION OR ENCLOSURES.

THANK YOU FOR YOUR INVALUABLE ASSISTANCE IN THIS INTERNSHIP PROGRAM AND
YOUR CONTRIBUTION TO OUR STUDENTS' EDUCATION.

1. Identify the general and specific roles and duties (observational, participatory, counseling, and so
   forth) assumed by the student, the overall responsibilities entrusted to the student, and the learning objectives established for the student.

2. Evaluate the student's ability to satisfy the objectives set forth for student interns by your agency.

Figure 6.5   Sample Student Internship Evaluation

3. Briefly describe the specific areas in which the student demonstrated particular abilities favorable to your profession.

4. In which areas would you suggest that the student concentrate his or her efforts to improve in order to achieve future success in the profession?

5. How would you rate the student's overall performance?
   Please circle one of the descriptions below:

   Excellent   Above average   Average   Below average   Poor

6. Did you discuss this evaluation with the student?

   Yes _____   No _____

Figure 6.5   (Cont.)

SUMMARY

The relationship between you and your agency supervisor serves as the medium through which you are able to make maximum use of the knowledge you bring to the placement and are helped to develop your skills and accept new concepts and ideas. Your agency supervisor should encourage you to discuss your feelings and attitudes about your work experiences and help you resolve work-related problems. He or she should also evaluate your progress—or lack thereof—*with you.* You should receive credit for what you are doing well and comments on needed areas of improvement.

It is not unusual for interns initially to feel a sense of dependence on their supervisors. During the course of your internship, your relationship with your agency supervisor will become less dependent and more reciprocal with an exchange of the supervisor's feedback and your input. The introduction to your peer support system will also contribute to a diminished feeling of dependence. Your peers will give you tremendous support by providing a sense of comradeship and valuable information on potential internship sites.

Further, during the internship, you will be afforded a primary (faculty) source of supervision. Faculty supervision is the fundamental instructional goal necessary for you to develop personally and professionally. The skills learned by achieving this goal will prove beneficial throughout your professional career. You will largely determine the amount of supervision that you need to strengthen your personal and professional development. Although this should be a mutual relationship between you and the faculty supervisor, the faculty supervisor is ultimately responsible for your preparedness and ability to carry out your obligations to the agency and the university. One key to positive career development is the ability to acknowledge the need for supervision and to acquire support when necessary. Another key is the ability to communicate effectively with the faculty supervisor by being honest and ethical. Finally, you should be familiar with grievance procedures, and if controversy regarding evaluations by the faculty supervisor or grades from the internship coordinator arises, comply with the university's grievance policies.

DISCUSSION QUESTIONS

1. What kind of relationship should a student strive for with his or her agency supervisor?
2. How can a student ensure a positive relationship with his or her agency supervisor?
3. How should assignments and grading be determined? Make sure you are familiar with your responsibilities.
4. How should grievances between students and agency supervisors be resolved?

7

Values and Ethical Standards

QUESTIONS FOR STUDENTS
How does your value system affect your attitude and behavior toward your clients?
Why do ethical guidelines exist?
What common ethical and moral dilemmas may you be faced with during your internship?

THE INTERN'S VALUE SYSTEM

What are your values, social principles, and standards? Your values will play an important role in how you adhere to the ethical standards set forth in the criminal justice system. Not only is it necessary for you to understand your own values, it is important for you to be openminded about the values of the agency's staff and clients. If you have negative feelings toward people who are involved in the criminal justice system, this may not be the place for you to intern or the profession for you to consider. You may dislike these people's lifestyles and values, but your feelings should not influence your professionalism.

During this internship, another part of your experience will be finding out more about yourself and evaluating or reevaluating your own values. For instance, you may consider yourself to be a broadminded person and be amazed to discover that you are experiencing feelings of prejudice and a reluctance to treat some clients impartially. Granted, this may be a painful lesson, but it may also be the most important lesson you learn during your internship, so you will "do no harm"—the first ethical rule of interning (Baird, 1996, p. 28). Once you recover from this bombshell, you may become more accepting of people with different values; if you cannot, you will not be effective with others. It is not unusual to have this experience, and sharing your feelings with your supervisors, other staff members, and peers can help you survive this trying time.

While interning in the criminal justice system, you may work with staff members who have become burned out and may try to influence you to adopt their skeptical and harsh attitudes toward clients. Because you will want to establish a good relationship with these staff members, you may find yourself in a situation that may compromise your values. When such a situation occurs, it is important not to let anyone influence your thinking. You will be more effective if you make your own assessments of others, and you will also ensure that you provide high-quality treatment and exhibit good ethical principles.

Below are three ethical situations that interns had to confront.

Student #1: I interned at a correctional facility for youthful offenders. From the very beginning of the internship, I encountered problems with my agency supervisor. The supervisor was often rude and sarcastic, making me very uncomfortable. The supervisor also treated the offenders in a disrespectful manner and encouraged me to "follow her lead." However, I was compelled to be respectful to all of the offenders as well as to the supervisor. I realized that the supervisor could hurt my grade on the midterm and final evaluations and my not conforming to her behavior could negatively affect my grade. I had no choice but to continue to act according to my value system no matter the consequences (Samuelson, 2002, p. 10).

Student #2: I interned at the Miami Halfway House, a residential treatment facility for juveniles. Although the agency supervisor was kind and professional, I experienced more unfavorable occurrences from certain members of the staff who seemed fed up with their careers. Furthermore, the clients, with their tendencies to disobey, often angered the staff. As a result, cursing and yelling often occurred at the facility. I, on the other hand, did not believe in this kind of treatment of the clients. They were coming out of situations like these at home, and I did not think that my field study would be successful with this type of approach. Nonetheless, certain staff members would often verbally express their surprise and annoyance that I could be so patient. I sometimes felt as if they were trying to bring me down to their aggravated level. I, however, did not submit to this "norm" and had a successful and enjoyable experience during my internship (Kazmierczak, 2003, p. 4).

Student #3: During my internship at a Department of Juvenile Justice Program, I heard a lot of negative comments and saw a lot of negative actions from staff members toward the offenders. I concluded that these negative actions were the results of the staff's exhaustion and burnout on the job. Some of the staff attempted to convince me to develop the same negative mind frame toward the offenders. Below are some examples of negative statements that staff made about certain offenders:

- "These boys will not survive in the outside world no more than two years, until they will be right back in another program if not prison."
- "I can see some dead five years from now."
- "Some will never amount to nothing once they leave this program."
- "Graduating from high school and getting a degree is the last thing on their minds." (Neely-Scott, 2003, p. 8)

After reading the above situations, how do you think you would have responded? What would you have done? How would you have felt?

ETHICAL PRINCIPLES FOR CRIMINAL JUSTICE PROFESSIONALS

Criminal justice is a multidisciplinary profession, consisting of judges, lawyers, psychiatrists, psychologists, social workers, and other helping professionals. As an intern, you may be working with an agency supervisor from any of these disciplines. To guarantee high-quality treatment and lessen the possibility of harm to clients, many professions have instituted formal ethical codes and principles. The states also attempt to shield clients by establishing laws to oversee the licensing and practice of many professions. Violations of these ethical codes and laws may result in the loss of the right to practice; for instance, a judge may be impeached and removed from the bench, or a psychiatrist may lose his or her license.

All professions do not have identical codes of ethics, but their codes share certain basic principles (Kitchener, 1984). The following are some of the codes under which many agency supervisors may be working:

- American Bar Association Code of Ethics
- American Counseling Association Code of Ethics and Standards of Practice
- Code of Ethical Principles for Marriage and Family Therapists
- Ethical Principles and Code of Conduct of Psychologists
- Ethical Standards for School Counselors
- NASW (National Association of Social Workers) Code of Ethics

The lack of a formal code of ethics or standards for the criminal justice system has become a matter of concern in teaching ethics in criminal justice. To address this issue, Kleinig and Smith (1997) edited a collection of invitational essays, originally presented at a workshop at John Jay College of Criminal Justice, on teaching criminal justice ethics. The authors of these essays, who are experts in practical and professional ethics, applied the knowledge they had gained from teaching in other areas, such as law, psychology, education, medicine, and social work, to criminal justice ethics. The questions they raised included the following: What should instructors be trying to achieve in teaching criminal justice ethics?

How best may they go about it? How can they tell if they have succeeded? It is hoped that the essays related to these questions will increase the resources available to instructors in integrating an ethics component into the criminal justice curriculum. Having been a social worker before I became a criminologist, I tend to use the NASW Code of Ethics. Some ethical issues that I have found most relevant for interns in my program are confidentiality, competence, corruption, and dual relationships. (See Figure 7.1 for a sample ethical agreement form.)

As an intern, you are expected to follow certain ethical guidelines for your benefit and protection, as well as for those of clients, internship supervisors and agencies, and the internship coordinator and university. Whenever you have questions about ethical conduct, you should discuss them with your agency supervisor or internship coordinator. The following are the minimum ethical standards that you, as an intern, must agree to follow:

CONFIDENTIALITY
Interns must not reveal the identity of clients or any information that would uncover the identity without written permission from the clients. There are two exceptions to this principle. The first is if the clients may be dangerous to themselves or others, and the second is in cases of the abuse and neglect of children and the elderly. In these situations, interns are required to inform their supervisors, who will contact the proper agencies and authorities. In some instances, courts can order the release of case notes and records. Interns should also become familiar with state laws. Confidentiality must also be maintained in the classroom when sharing information from cases.

COMPETENCY
Interns must acknowledge the limitations of their abilities to assist clients. It is imperative that they accept that some situations are beyond their experience and obtain assistance from their agency supervisors and employees.

CORRUPTION
Interns must not be involved in any illegal operations or violations of laws. They should not take part in any attempt to undermine the criminal justice system or abuse the power, given by the state, associated with their internships. Interns have a duty to report any mis-management of justice noticed while they are interning. They are obligated to treat all clients with justice and equity.

INTERPERSONAL RELATIONSHIPS
Interns will not develop a clinical relationship with anyone with whom they have an existing relationship of any type. It is unethical for interns to see classmates, co-workers, friends, or family members as clients. It is also unethical for them to become sexually or romantically involved with agency clients. Interns will not be involved in sexual harassment. I hereby agree to follow the guidelines stated above. I will also become familiar with the ethical guidelines for the professional discipline associated with the internship placement agency.

Signature of Intern _____ **Date** _____

Figure 7.1   Sample Ethical Agreement Form

Confidentiality

What is confidentiality? It is the principle that clients have the right to determine who will have access to information about them and their treatment and other privileged information, such as their criminal histories. In many mental health agencies, confidentiality is considered the primary ethical responsibility. However, the issues and limits of confidentiality vary from agency to agency.

As an intern, you will be expected to adhere to certain ethical guidelines for your benefit and protection, as well as those of clients, internship supervisors and agencies, and the internship coordinator and university. Whenever you have questions about ethical conduct, you should discuss them with your agency supervisor or internship coordinator.

If you are involved in counseling during your internship, your clients need to believe that their identities and the information they share will be released only with their permission (most agencies provide release-of-information forms for this purpose). Without this guarantee, clients are reluctant to express their thoughts and feelings openly. The only acceptable instances for breaching confidentiality are cases in which you have evidence that clients may be dangerous to themselves or others or are abusing or neglecting children or the elderly. In such situations, you should know your agency's policy and legal requirements for informing appropriate organizations. You need to become acquainted with particular legal proceedings that require case notes and other records to be released by order of the courts. If clients know that the courts can subpoena their records, they may be reluctant to share certain information, which may disrupt the treatment process (Nowell and Spruill, 1993). On the other hand, if clients are to make informed decisions, they should know the limits to confidentiality. Therefore, you must learn and follow the confidentiality policies of your agency and the laws of your state. When presenting and discussing case information in class, you must make sure that you maintain confidentiality. For instance, never use a client's name (or any other identifiable information) in written reports or oral presentations.

When interning at a criminal justice agency, you are responsible for inquiring about the issues and limits of confidentiality established by the agency and state laws. In this setting, you will probably be exposed to privileged information that you should not discuss outside the agency. For instance, if you are interning at a police department and are privileged to information regarding a raid, your discussion of it with friends, classmates, or family members may endanger the officers and jeopardize the raid. On the other hand, if you are interning in a state or federal prison, the policy on confidentiality or the state law may dictate that you must report certain information you receive, such as an escape that is being planned. If, while you are interning as a probation officer, a client informs you that he or she has violated probation (for example, by leaving the state without permission), you should know if the policy on confidentiality requires that you inform your agency supervisor.

As an intern, it will not always be obvious to you how much of the information on clients you should share with your supervisor and co-workers. After orientation, whether you are given your own caseload or are sharing a co-worker's, you should ask your supervisor how much and what type of information on clients you need to share with the original caseworker, and even with the supervisor, before you begin to work with clients.

There has been an ongoing debate in the field regarding confidentiality. According to Clairborn et al. (1994), some studies have found that clients and the general public believe that confidentiality should never be breached. However, the respondents in Rubanowitz's (1987) study maintained that there are certain situations, usually involving knowledge of the possibility or actual commission of a crime, in which a client's confidentiality should be violated and appropriate authorities should be advised.

Of all the ethical and legal issues faced by helping professionals, confidentiality is the one that is most constantly considered a source of moral dilemmas (Pope and Vetter, 1992; Stadler and Paul, 1986). Because of the perceived significance of confidentiality and the frequency of moral dilemmas associated with it, you must fully understand its standards. In doing so, you will be able to avoid violating the standards through thoughtlessness.

The next sections discuss some general issues of confidentiality that apply to most clinical situations and criminal justice agencies. These issues are included only as general guidelines, so you must be certain that they can be helpful in your particular agency. If you are interning at an agency that serves minors, such as a juvenile detention facility or a drug and alcohol treatment facility that practices group and/or family therapy, be aware that certain therapy techniques present unique issues and that these guidelines may not be appropriate to protect confidentiality in these settings (Paradise and Kirby, 1990; Vesper and Brock, 1990).

Release-of-Information Forms

Standard release-of-information forms to protect confidentiality are used by most agencies. (See Figure 7.2 for a sample form.) These are important forms that clients must sign before any written or verbal information about them can be released. The forms usually provide a place for listing the persons or organizations who are authorized to receive the information; the date of the release; the period during which the release of information is valid; the reason for the release; the precise details requested for release; the form of communication (written or verbal) for the release; the name of the client; the name of the person authorized to release the information (usually the therapist or supervisor); and finally, the signatures of the client and the therapist or supervisor (Bennett et al., 1990).

Customarily, if anyone contacts you by telephone or e-mail or visits you at the agency, declaring that he or she has the client's consent to discuss the client's

This form authorizes the release and sharing of information
between _____
         (Intern's agency)

and _____
         (Organization requesting the information)

with regard to the client named below. The signing of this release form by the person/guardian allows the above-named agencies to share with each other relevant information about the client. This information is limited to referral information, psychological test reports, medical records, arrest records, and recommendations for treatment. It may be in the form of written reports or conversation in person or by telephone. This permission can be terminated—in writing or verbally—at any time by the client.

PLEASE *PRINT* THE NAME OF THE CLIENT _____

_____   _____
Client's Signature (Guardian)   Date

_____   _____
Authorized Signature (Supervisor)   Date

Figure 7.2 Sample Release-of-Information Form

case or see the client's files but is not listed on the release form (or the client has not signed a release form), you must not even admit that the person is a client, much less share the files or discuss the case. If the person is insistent, the best way to handle the situation without acknowledging that the person is a client is to say something like this: "I am unable to share any information that may be retained by this agency without written consent. I am sure you are aware of the importance of confidentiality, and I will be happy to assist you with whatever information I can once I receive a release of information."

If the person continues to demand information, you should refer him or her to your supervisor. Do not allow yourself to be pressured into providing *any* information without the release-of-information form.

Protecting Files

To protect files and guarantee the confidentiality of records, you should store all case notes and any other relevant information in *locked* file cabinets. It is good practice to keep cabinets locked any time you are away from their location, especially overnight. You should never leave your notes or any other records that identify clients where they may be accidentally seen by other agency employees or the general public. A supplementary safeguard used by many agencies is to stamp "Confidential" on all case records. If your agency has converted the paper files to computer files, you should never leave the computer screen on in your absence, thereby allowing others to gain access to the files.

If one of your assignments as an intern is to keep a journal, you should be careful not to lose or misplace it. As a precaution, I tell my interns who keep journals to mask the clients' identities by using fake names or initials. It is a good practice to avoid using only first names because of the possibility that they may be associated with actual clients.

Information Sharing among Co-workers

By now, it should be clear that no information should be shared with outside sources without a release-of-information form from your client. But what about sharing information with your co-workers? This issue of confidentiality is not as clear-cut. Baird (1996) suggested that before you share information on a client with another agency employee, you should ask yourself: Who is the person? Why does he (or she) want the information? What information is being requested? Where are you (public or private setting)? When should you discuss the information? How will you share the information? (See Box 7.1.) Instant and spontaneous

---

BOX 7.1   *Sharing Information with Colleagues*

Guidelines for sharing information with outside sources are relatively clear and the rule can be summarized succinctly as "Not without written permission from the client." Questions about sharing information with colleagues within an internship placement are not as easily answered. As each setting and situation are different, it may be helpful to offer a general framework you can use to help make your decisions. This framework revolves around the "W" question words: who, why, what, where, when, and how. Before sharing information about a client with anyone, you should ask yourself:

1. Who is the person? Has the client given permission for them to have the information? What is his or her role or authority within the clinical setting? What professional training does he or she have? What is his or her relationship to the client? What do you think of his or her clinical skills, ethical knowledge, etc.? Also ask yourself if the other person knows about and respects the principle of confidentiality.

2. Why does the person want the information? Is he or she involved in the client's treatment in some way? Or just curious? Is he or she seeking

information to help him or her understand the client, or is he or she likely to use it in a counterproductive way?

3. What information is being requested? Is the person asking for data such as address, phone, etc., or is he or she asking for clinical information about the nature of the client's concerns or background? Is he or she asking for general impressions from tests or interviews, or does he or she want specific scores or answers to specific questions? Remember that merely because someone is asking for a certain type of information does not mean that you should provide the information requested. Depending on the circumstances, you may choose to offer summaries or general impressions rather than specific test results or interview responses. You may also choose to offer no information at all if there is a probability that it will not be used responsibly and professionally.

4. Where are you? Is the setting private, or are you in a public place where others could easily overhear your discussion? Are the office doors closed? Could people in the waiting room hear you? Are other clients nearby?

5. When should you discuss the information? Is now the best time to share information? Will you have adequate time to discuss and explain things or will you be rushed and not do an adequate job? Would it be better to schedule a specific time and place rather than sharing things in passing?

6. How will you share the information? Is it best to discuss information directly one on one, or can you accomplish the task over the phone? Should you formalize the exchange of information in writing, either by providing the information itself in written form or by keeping notes of the conversation? What are the relative pros and cons of direct verbal versus written exchange?

If you ask these questions immediately and automatically each time you consider sharing information about a client, the chances of carelessness will be reduced significantly.

Source: Brian N. Baird, Department of Psychology, Pacific Lutheran University, Tacoma, Washington, 1996.

self-examination of these questions whenever you consider sharing information with co-workers may help you decrease the mistakes you may make in issues of confidentiality.

Abuse

Several state laws require health professionals and educators to report cases of suspected or known child abuse or neglect (Swenson, 1993), as well as cases of the neglect or abuse of elderly persons. As an intern, if you are working with a child or elderly person who informs you that he or she is being physically or sexually abused or if there is physical evidence that abuse has taken place, you are required to inform your supervisor, who, in turn, is obligated to inform the proper agencies or authorities. The agency that investigates claims and intercedes for the protection of the child is usually called Child Protective Services, a branch of the Department of Social Services in a city or county. The same department also investigates claims of elderly abuse and neglect.

In an extensive review of legal and clinical concerns connected with child neglect and abuse, Howing and Wodarski (1992) stated that because of the frequency of child abuse, it is probable that helping professionals will be confronted with instances of suspected abuse. Because the laws differ from state to state and because of vagueness in the law, it is sometimes difficult to know when to report.

Despite these difficulties, most states that require child neglect and abuse to be reported provide protection from civil liability (being sued) if the reports are submitted in good will and without animosity. Negligence in reporting, however, may result in criminal or civil lawsuits (Howing and Wodarski, 1992).

Thus, early in your internship, you should ask your supervisor to inform you about the agency's policy and the state law on reporting neglect and abuse. Be aware that the accusation of abuse is serious, and you should not be quick to report a case without investigating it (under agency supervision); nevertheless, if your supervisor thinks there are legitimate reasons, the abuse must be reported to the proper authorities. It would also be advisable to inform your internship coordinator that you have reported the incident to your agency supervisor.

Competence

During your internship training, you will need to monitor your ethical behavior continuously and deliberately. Doing so will help you operate at *your* level of competence—another important standard of most codes of ethics.

In time, you may become as skilled at performing some of the same tasks as your co-workers and may be viewed as more competent by your supervisor and agency employees. However, you may still face situations about which you are uncertain. Therefore, it is crucial for you to recognize the extent and limitations of your skills and ask for help from your supervisor when you need it. For example, a client who is contemplating suicide will not be within your ability to handle, no matter how much you may want to help the client, and must be reported to your supervisor immediately. Always be aware that good intentions cannot replace competence and that there will be times when you will not be the best judge of your capabilities and behavior.

You may be unaware of several factors that must be weighed in evaluating specific situations, such as formal and informal agency policies (which are discussed in Chapter 6) or policies of other criminal justice agencies that must be considered. Consulting with your co-workers and supervisor is a good policy to follow, both during your internship and after you become a professional.

There are several reasons why clients are reassigned to other agency employees. Many times, the clients need special attention or specific services that are not immediately recognized, and your supervisor may have to assign them to workers who are more skilled in these particular areas. This happened with one of my interns, who felt much better when the supervisor advised him that the client needed the skills of a substance abuse counselor, which the intern did not have. The most important lesson you can learn during your internship is how much *you do not know*. This learning process will continue into your professional career, and you should never be too proud or ashamed to seek assistance. Even after several years of work experience, supervision will play a primary role in your professional training. After I received a master's degree in social work, I had to have five years of supervised training before I could apply for state certification, which would allow me to participate in unsupervised counseling. In addition, to keep state certification and maintain my practice as a family counselor, I had to have my case notes reviewed monthly by a certified social worker who had been practicing at least ten years.

Because professionals recognize that there is always new information, and hence the need for continuous study, most states require some form of continuing education credits to obtain and maintain certification and licensing. In the criminal justice field, you will be expected continually to acquire knowledge by reading professional journals and attending various conferences related to your area of specialization and consult with other professionals with greater skills in that area.

In concluding this discussion of competence, I want to emphasize that interns are held responsible for their actions just as professionals are; it is this fact that interns do not always realize. For instance, one of my students who was working in child protective services was instructed by her supervisor to take an infant to a foster care home; instead, she took the infant to her home overnight and was charged with kidnapping. Her supervisor and I, as her internship coordinator, could also have been held responsible for the intern's actions. However, we were not, and with our support, she was placed on probation, but not allowed to complete her internship with the agency. This student, acting in a professional role and given primary responsibility for the infant's care, should have been aware that it was her responsibility to follow the same legal and ethical standards as those of a professional (Zakutansky and Sirles, 1993).

One of the basic rules I stress with my students regarding their levels of competence is "Do no harm." It is natural for you to want to accept challenges, appreciating that your success will increase your confidence, elevate your self-esteem, and improve your skills. But this need must be secondary; your primary concern must be the consequences of your actions for your clients.

Corruption

Although it is unlikely that you will be involved in situations in which you must deal with corruption as an intern, it is possible that you may encounter corruption, since this issue has been considered a frequent problem for the criminal justice system. Corruption occurs when a person uses his or her official position to obtain personal profit. In some cases, interns work (as you may do) in an official role that is formally defined by the agency's organizational structure. During the years of my program, only one student reported being involved in corruption. He said: "While on a ride-along, I observed a suspect confess to stealing several season ticket packages for sports events. Before booking the suspect, the arresting officers 'pocketed the tickets.' Later they offered me a package and I accepted because I was afraid to refuse."

Obviously, this is a clear-cut example of corruption. But sometimes the issue is not so clear. For example, while interning, would you be comfortable accepting free meals or free passes to musical or sports events or other gifts? Even though your agency may not provide clear-cut policies regarding these and similar situations, they may fit into the ethically gray area of corruption. In such cases, your value system will influence your response. However, it will not always be easy to adhere to your value system when your peers pressure you to overlook your values. For example, as a police intern, you may be determined never to be involved in police brutality, but when invited by your supervisor or other officers to participate, you may find that your need for acceptance may come into conflict with your values. One of my interns was confronted with a similar situation. Because his value system would not allow him to participate, he felt he would be evaluated unfairly by his supervisor and alienated by other officers, so he requested and received a transfer to another agency. At all times, you must keep in mind that you are learning to be a professional, and as an intern, you will occasionally make mistakes and use poor judgment. These mistakes can be minimized, however, if you have frequent discussions with your peers, agency supervisor, and internship coordinator.

Dual Relationships

If, as an intern, you are providing counseling, professional ethics forbid the establishment of *dual relationships*. Boryrs and Pope (1989) and Kitchener (1988) reported that even though dual relationships include a broad range of interactions, the underlying ethical standard and primary concern is that as a counselor, you must avoid any involvement with your client that could jeopardize the healing process. For example, functioning as a counselor for another intern at your agency would be considered a dual relationship. An even more serious and damaging form of dual relationship would be your involvement in a romantic or sexual relationship with your client. This issue is addressed later in this section.

Kagle and Giebelhausen (1994) and Baird (1996) noted that the risk involved in dual relationships is the probability that counselors may, intentionally or unintentionally, allow some facet of their nonprofessional relationships to disrupt their counseling relationships. Gutheil and Gabbard (1993) pointed out that what may initially be seen as a slight departure from usual procedures may eventually lead to more significant violations.

In some instances, clients have been responsible for initiating dual relationships. If you are ever confronted with this situation, it is your responsibility to handle the matter in an ethical manner. The best rule for avoiding dual relationships is never to provide counseling for anyone with whom you share an existing relationship.

As an intern, when associating with agency clients and co-workers, you should conduct yourself in a professional manner, which will help you develop and maintain appropriate relationships. Avoid the temptation to begin a personal relationship with a client outside the agency because the situation could lead to circumstances that may cause you to compromise your values and ethics. One of my interns, working in a federal prison camp without a fence and with open access to the roadway, assisted an inmate who was slipping out for the night, with the intention of returning before morning roll call, by giving him a ride to the nearest bar. When the intern was released from her placement, she stated: "He was already out; I just gave him a lift." Of course, that was the end of that internship. The issue that concerned both me and her field supervisor was that she felt she had done nothing to warrant her release from the placement. In this case the intern obviously developed a personal relationship with the inmate that clouded her values and had a negative impact on her professional conduct. With all the media attention on unethical romantic and sexual conduct, it should be obvious that these relationships are the most harmful and legally significant models of dual relationships. The ethical codes of all helping professional organizations specially forbid sexual relations with clients (Kagle and Giebelhausen, 1994); nevertheless, these relationships continue to occur. The neglect of this standard has created much trouble for many professionals, tremendous stress for their families, and severe and permanent harm to the people they desired to help.

Another situation is when an intern consents to a sexual relationship with an agency supervisor. Who is guilty of sexual misconduct? The agency supervisor is in the role of mentor and role model and usually grades the intern. Because of the unequal distribution of power in this relationship, the intern's consent to participate in unethical activities does not relieve the supervisor of responsibility for unprofessional actions (Walsh, 1990). If you are approached by an agency employee, there are several creative ways of dealing with these sexual advances. One that has worked for other interns is to tell the person that the professional code of ethics prohibits intimacy between interns and co-workers.

In addition to professional organizations' codes of ethics, several states also have laws regarding sexual misconduct that make it not only an ethical issue, but a criminal matter, such as the example of sexual harassment given above (Strasburger Jorgenson, and Randel, 1991). After reviewing the existing laws, Applebaum (1990) reported that in many instances the breach of this ethical standard is considered a felony and may result in imprisonment and fines. There is also little protection from civil lawsuits (Jorgenson, Randel, and Strasburger, 1991).

JUSTICE, EQUALITY, AND PUNISHMENT

Whatever occurs at your internship placement, recognize it as one experience. Do not judge all agencies, employees, clients, or yourself by this limited experience. Valuable lessons can be learned from even the worst environments, from the most trying clients, and the most unhealthy staff members. You may, indeed, have experiences during your internship that may disappoint or distress you. However, this is not a good reason to quit the internship or conclude that it is not a good learning experience.

While you are interning as a student of criminal justice, criminology, or related courses, your classroom experience, academic assignments, and the media will influence the formation of your values regarding the criminal justice system. Your comprehension derived from these experiences will be exposed to the realities of the administration of justice and of the people who are administering this justice.

Your internship is the time when you will anticipate transferring theory into practice. On some occasions, however, you may think that what was presented in the classroom does not apply to the *real world* of the criminal justice system. I mentioned earlier that one of my interns witnessed a case of police brutality. He wanted to report it, but did not, and asked to be transferred to another agency. This was his first encounter with the reality that unjust and unfair administration of justice by *professionals* in the criminal justice system does exist. Therefore, in some cases, their actions may be detrimental to clients, their agency, and you if it meets their needs. Another intern of mine, while working as a legal assistant at the Office of the State Attorney, was infuriated to learn the extent to which plea-bargaining was applied to felony cases (assault, rape, battery, etc.). After assisting and observing the attorney commit so many hours to case presentations and involvement in plea-bargaining, at the end of the internship she decided not to apply to law school.

The lesson she learned was that even well-intentioned programs, as plea-bargaining was created to be, run by healthy, caring people, do not always work efficiently or properly. Many times, the greatest efforts by the most considerate people are obstructed by faulty programs. These are two examples of the fact that the administration of justice is not always honorable or equitable. As an intern you may be exposed to what the profession considers bargain and street justice. Involvement in these situations will usually create ethical or moral predicaments with which you must grapple. You will be confronted with how to deal with the situations, and you will examine your responsibility in them.

Although there are no cut-and-dried rules on how to handle unjust and unfair situations, it is suggested that you not interefere at the scene for fear that you might magnify a potentially dangerous situation. It is also recommended that you discuss the situation with your internship coordinator for assistance managing the same or a similar situation.

If you become disturbed by an immoral or unlawful situation, first discuss it with your internship coordinator, who will help you decide whether to take the issue to your agency supervisor or co-worker. In any event, be aware that your internship may be in jeopardy if you decide to confront a co-worker or your agency supervisor.

My students have received mixed responses to their reports of unethical or illegal incidences. Whereas some reports have been well received, others have not, and the consequences have been negative. For example, one intern, observing a co-worker making frequent trips to the restroom, thought the person was ill and followed her in. She discovered the co-worker taking drugs and reported the incident to her agency supervisor, even though she thought she might be ostracized by her fellow employees. Because this was a drug-free workplace, however, the agency supervisor and the other employees appreciated her report about the employees who was acting in an unprofessional and illegal way. On the other hand, another intern working in a correctional facility was ostracized by his fellow employees when he reported an incident of sexual misconduct between an inmate and a staff member.

Even though the issues of justice, equity, and punishment must be addressed, most interns gain a strong sense of accomplishment and satisfaction from their internships. They enjoy the opportunity to work with remarkable clients and to encounter healthy, caring professionals whom they come to admire and are pleased with their work and their learning experience, as you will be.

SUMMARY

Your personal values greatly influence your loyalty to the ethical guidelines of the criminal justice system. To be an asset to the criminal justice system while interning, you must understand your own value system and accept different values held by your clients and agency staff members. You must be open to learning more about yourself and evaluating and reevaluating your values. You should never sacrifice your values to establish good rapport with your peers, co-workers, or agency supervisor.

Ethical guidelines exist to safeguard the well-being of clients, professionals, and professions. As an intern, it is your responsibility to be well informed about the ethical standards instituted by your profession and the agency in which you are interning and to discuss them with your agency supervisor and internship coordinator. In this chapter we have examined important ethical issues that are relevant to you as an intern.

During your internship, you may witness incidences in which clients are being treated unjustly and unfairly. You may also observe co-workers and/or supervisors involved in immoral and illegal activities. These situations exist, and you will be affected by the ethical dilemmas they create. Learning how to deal appropriately with these difficulties is a crucial part of your learning experience and your professional development.

DISCUSSION QUESTIONS

1. How will your individual value system affect your progress during your internship?

2. Why is it important to follow a certain ethical standard guideline while in the criminal justice field?

3. How can a student ensure the fairest treatment of the clients, the agency, and him- or herself? What issues must be considered?

4. How should an intern act in an immoral or unethical situation?

PART III

Evaluation and Future Careers

Now that you know the various aspects of field placements, such as your role as an intern, the roles of the faculty coordinator and the agency supervisor, and the importance of values and ethical standards, it is time to assess your internship experience, to think of your future career, and to use the resource guide located in the back of this book to locate and contact several criminal justice agencies in twenty-five major cities in the United States.

The following chapters will help you evaluate your internship experience and set future career goals. Chapter 8 will assist you in evaluating your total field educational experience, and in Chapter 9 we provide invaluable information regarding your professional future in the career field or graduate education. These chapters also discuss several things that you have to do to complete your internship relationships with your supervisor, peers, and other co-workers.

Now that you are near the end of your internship, a significant component of the procedure for terminating your field placement is the review process that you and your field supervisor undergo. In this process, you and your supervisor should allot adequate time to discuss your personal and professional development and any areas in which you need additional work.

CHAPTER

8

Evaluation of Field Education Experience

QUESTIONS FOR STUDENTS

Did you make the desired progress on your original internship goals?

What strengths and weaknesses did you discover during your field experience?

How has this experience influenced your future goals?

EVALUATION OF PERSONAL AND PROFESSIONAL PROGRESS

The traditional way to measure your progress is by filling out some type of evaluation form, as discussed in Chapter 6. Although your internship coordinators have probably asked that these reports be sent directly to them to help them determine your grades, you and your agency supervisor should first review these reports and jointly discuss your views and opinions. In our program, three seminars are scheduled during the semester. The purpose of the first meeting is for the interns to become acquainted with each other and the internship coordinator and for the internship coordinator to provide a syllabus and direction for the course during the semester. At the second (midterm) meeting, the interns share their experiences with their placements, and they discuss their midterm evaluations and progress to date received from the agency supervisors. The third meeting again focuses on shared experiences and group and individual discussions of the final evaluations and progress toward the interns' goals for personal and professional growth. In addition, weekly informal individual sessions are held to discuss goals and learning objectives, which provide more clear-cut areas for evaluating the field experiences. At these meetings, the interns take notes to assist them with their final self-evaluations.

The hardest part of the evaluation process is probably learning to accept critical feedback effectively. It is natural for you to want to hear only compliments and praise from your coordinator and supervisor, and they would prefer to give you glowing evaluations. Although praise is important because it increases your self-esteem and gives you the strength and faith to persevere, constructive criticism is vital because it establishes essential directions for further personal and professional development. Therefore, it is recommended that you welcome constructive criticism as a means of identifying and setting future goals. Baird (1966) suggested that one way to learn to accept criticism constructively is to write a self-evaluation in which you identify things you did well during your internship and areas in which you recognize that you need to improve. This exercise will help you see your strengths and weaknesses before the joint review and better accept and process critical feedback. Furthermore, self-evaluation can become a regular practice of personal reflection that will be useful throughout your career.

It is important to record carefully, for later reflection, how much you have changed personally and professionally during your internship. If you keep a journal, as suggested in Chapter 6, you will have evidence to support your intuitive feeling of having gained a great deal. During your internship, several factors have interacted to help you accomplish the goals and objectives that you set out to gain from your field education experience, and your initial impressions of your internship experience are significant for assessing your personal growth and professional progress. For instance, your peers', agency supervisors', and co-workers' expectations of you can be crucial assessment factors. Your internship may have been the first opportunity you have had to satisfy the expectations of experts in your desired profession. Assessing how well you have met others' expectations, as well as your own, is an important part of self-evaluation.

FIELD SUPERVISOR'S EVALUATION

Interns are usually evaluated by both their agency supervisors and faculty internship coordinators according to criteria they receive before their internships began. In our program, agency supervisors give students this information during initial interviews in the semester before the internships take place, and (as the faculty internship coordinator) I give them a syllabus containing my requirements and evaluation criteria in the first seminar meeting during the first week of their internships. (See Chapter 6 for a sample syllabus and criteria for the required term paper.) Although expectations and requirements may vary, there are some common areas of evaluation.

Most agency supervisors' expectations are based on their experiences with interns and facilitating the personal and professional development of other agency employees. These expectations are usually broad based because the experiences and expectations of internships are different and the personal goals of interns vary.

At the beginning of your internship, you should ask your faculty internship coordinator or agency supervisor if there are established guidelines for evaluation; if there are, you should review the guidelines immediately to make sure that you understand what is expected of you. It has been my experience that some agencies, particularly those that are implementing their first internship programs, do not have an established format for evaluation. Consequently, I automatically give the interns I supervise a broad-based sample of a fixed-format evaluation during our first seminar meeting. If your supervisor does not have a fixed format for evaluation, review the sample evaluation presented in Chapter 6. Here are some specific areas that most supervisors are concerned about:

1. **Reliability and Dependability** Your supervisor will evaluate you on such things as dress, punctuality, attendance, constructive use of time, completion of assignments, and completion of required internship hours.

2. **Ethical Knowledge and Behavior** Your supervisor will probably inform you of the agency's ethical guidelines. As an intern, you will be expected to develop (or already have) knowledge of general ethical guidelines, know the ethical guidelines of the agency, demonstrate your insights into and sensitivity for ethical concerns, and display personal conduct compatible with ethical guidelines. (See Chapter 7 for ethical principles in the field.)

3. **Level of Knowledge and Learning Ability** You will be evaluated on your knowledge of the client population at the beginning and end of your internship and on your ability to learn and process new information and apply new information in your agency setting.

4. **Receptiveness to Supervision** You will be evaluated on how receptive you are to feedback and recommendations from your supervisor and your active participation in obtaining the required supervision. Again, your willingness to explore personal strengths and weaknesses will be weighed, as will the effectiveness of your implementation of your supervisor's recommendations.

5. **Interaction with Clients** Your ability to interact well with clients is an important consideration. The criteria will include your level of comfort while interacting with clients, how effectively you communicate during interactions, and your sensitivity to clients' needs and cultural and gender differences.

6. **Socialization with Co-workers** The ability to be relaxed while interacting with other agency personnel, to communicate effectively while relating information and verbalizing your views, and to obtain information and opinions from your co-workers are important aspects of your professional development and meaningful elements for evaluation.

7. **Workmanship** The quality of your performance in keeping credible and precise records; in maintaining reliable, factually correct, and professionally composed reports; and in presenting articulate verbal narratives that are administratively useful will have a strong influence on your evaluation.

8. **Aptitude for the Profession** The caliber of your overall accomplishments during your internship and the extent of your personal and professional growth will contribute greatly to assessments of your aptitude for working in your profession. At the conclusion of the internship, you and your supervisor may determine that you are a good candidate for working in the field represented by the agency. On the other hand, the experience may cause you to rethink your professional goals and to begin to pursue other areas. Some of my students have stated that they would rather find out at this time in their lives that they need to change career paths rather than to make this discovery after completing their degrees. Therefore, be aware that one important purpose of an internship is to discover where *you do not wish to work,* as well as where you do.

FIELD-SITE EVALUATION

As part of their internship assignments, my students are required to assess their agencies on the basis of how well the agencies met their internship goals. Some students have also evaluated agencies on how well the agencies' goals and objectives were met, on the basis of the discussion in Chapter 4. Even though your faculty coordinator will make site visits, it is impossible to know how conducive the internship experience is to your desired educational outcome. For this reason, your faculty coordinator will be interested in your opinions about how well the agency met your expectations and goals and whether future interns should be placed there. This evaluation will also benefit you in the future when you consider employment opportunities. One intern evaluated the placement site this way:

> Overall I really enjoyed my experience as an intern. In my agency [Federal Bureau of Prisons], I learned about the behind-the-scenes part of criminal justice. I didn't have any hands-on experience with inmates. Since my office deals with the paperwork, not with the inmates themselves, I could not really see how most of the criminological theories I learned in class applied in the real world. I could not see how programs affect the inmates or why the inmates may have committed the crimes. It is hard to understand these things when you never actually meet the inmates. . . .

> I wish to state that I have enjoyed other aspects of this experience. I have learned a lot and made some valuable contacts in the criminal justice system. I would recommend this internship to anyone who wants to learn about the behind-the-scenes part of criminal justice. It would be especially valuable for someone who is interested in community corrections. However, I would not recommend this internship to someone who wants hands-on experience.

This was a first-time placement, and this brief statement helped me determine the type of students who would benefit from it. The following statement by another intern indicates that even though the agency lacked sufficient resources, the placement was beneficial:

> As a result of my internship placement with the Guardian Ad Litem Program, my criminological understanding has been greatly clarified and challenged in terms of actual criminal justice-related work. I was able to observe firsthand things that I only read about in textbooks and to participate in judicial court proceedings, which gave me the experience of seeing the manner in which a judge in delinquency proceedings reaches certain rulings. I also noticed the different styles and attitudes that the judges brought to their roles and how they affected their decisions and the behavior of other agency workers. . . .
>
> Several flaws were also evident in and around the agency. The main flaw was the computer system network. For an agency that has between 28 and 83 workers a day, only five computers were available. One computer is usually not even open for use on a regular basis. Also, audio and video equipment, which is necessary for training sessions, is either outdated or experiences many operational difficulties. However, these flaws are not enough to offset the overall positive experience. The GAL program is, in my opinion, of superior quality given the number of workers and volunteers it has. It truly makes a difference in the lives of children.

As an intern, you may be hesitant to share your opinions with agency staff; however, your impressions are usually appreciated because they bring a new outlook to the issues.

FACULTY COORDINATOR'S EVALUATION

During your internship, your faculty coordinator might pay two to three site visits to your agency, depending on the number of interns placed for the semester. These visits, which are usually spread throughout the semester (beginning, midterm, and end), although informative, do not provide ample opportunity for field evaluations. Consequently, the faculty coordinator's evaluation is determined largely by the field supervisor's evaluations. Some faculty coordinators may supplement their evaluation criteria, as I do, with a required observation-participation term paper.

Because of the restrictions on actual observation, your faculty coordinator may evaluate and grade you on the basis of his or her personal standards applied to interns; your participation in seminars and weekly informal discussions; your journal entries; the quality of your term paper, if applicable; and your field supervisor's evaluation.

Some students have informed me that they have been asked to evaluate their agency supervisors and to suggest ways in which the supervisory process could be improved. If this request is made of you, realize that the process not only helps your supervisor but allows you to practice giving sincere feedback. The reciprocal exchange of opinions can be beneficial to both you and your supervisor in bringing better closure to your relationship and the internship. If you are given this opportunity, remember the earlier discussion on giving and receiving constructive criticism. Also because of the authority your supervisor has over you, you must consider carefully whether to articulate any negative statements to your supervisor. The University of Miami has eliminated this problem for students in evaluating all faculty by requiring that the evaluation process be completed in the absence of faculty and the results withheld until after the grading period.

RELATING THE FIELD EXPERIENCE TO FUTURE CAREERS

Many colleges and universities have career planning and placement centers with high-quality resources to help students attain future career goals relative to internship experiences, whether the goal is to find a full-time job upon graduation or to attend graduate school. An effective career planning process begins on your first day on campus and continues throughout your college years, including your internship, if you take advantage of the numerous workshops, panel discussions, career fairs, and presentations of information presented by on-campus recruiters. Being an active participant in these events will afford you the knowledge and opportunity to connect your internship experience to your future career.

SUMMARY

This chapter focused on the evaluation process, and we discussed how to measure your personal growth and professional development during your internship. It also described how your field supervisor and faculty internship coordinator appraise you and gave some insight into how you may appraise your internship site.

Assessments by your field supervisor and faculty coordinator are reliable indicators of your personal and professional growth, as well as your potential as a criminal justice professional. Furthermore, some supervisors think feedback should be bilateral and encourage interns to give their honest opinions on the ways that supervision can be enhanced in the future. If you are afforded this opportunity, remember that there is a natural imbalance in the authoritative arrangement of the supervisor-intern relationship, so you should consider carefully voicing any negative opinions to your supervisor.

Evaluating your experiences should be a continuous process and should not just occur when you leave the agency at the end of your internship. A detailed evaluation of your internship experiences will make them more meaningful. Self-evaluation, honestly appraising your accomplishments, is one of the most meaningful skills that you can cultivate during your internship because it will contribute greatly to your future growth and development in whatever profession you enter after college.

DISCUSSION QUESTIONS

1. How should a student evaluate him or herself? It is crucial for the student to be able to determine how his or her individual field study experience challenged and improved his or her knowledge of that particular aspect of the criminal justice system.

2. What factors should a field supervisor consider upon evaluating the intern? Make sure that you talk these evaluations over to ensure fairness and valid reasons for particular assessments.

3. How does the faculty coordinator evaluate his or her students? How is the field supervisor's evaluation relevant to the overall outcome?

4. How does an internship aid in obtaining a career in the future?

9

Future Careers

What kind of job do you want?
How would you plan a job search?
Do you plan to attend professional school?

PREPARING TO CHOOSE

Most students who take criminal justice internships are usually interested in careers in such disciplines as the law, law enforcement, corrections, and juvenile justice. While interning and after your placement has ended, you will be confronted with decisions regarding your future career goals. To make these decisions, you will need to ask yourself several questions, such as these: Was the workplace conducive to being productive? Did I enjoy working with the clients? Would I want to continue working in the same type of agency? Do I have the credentials, or am I willing to obtain the credentials needed to obtain a position with the agency? These are only a few of the many questions you will need to consider to set realistic career goals. These questions indicate that there are several steps that you must take in setting your careers goals: (1) discovering the types of positions that are appropriate for your skills, (2) locating those positions, (3) composing a résumé that will entice people to employ you, (4) obtaining interviews, (5) preparing for interviews, and (6) determining whether particular positions and organizations will contribute to your personal and professional growth. In this chapter we provide some information that will help you consider these and other factors related to obtaining a position in your chosen field.

DETERMINING VOCATIONAL ASPIRATIONS

The first step in determining your vocational aspirations is to find out what kind of job you want. When making this decision, consider that the work you choose should be interesting and challenging, should make use of your professional skills and abilities, and should provide educational opportunities for professional growth. The first step in finding out what kind of job you want is to take a personal assessment of yourself. In this assessment you should consider your personal likes and dislikes and how important maximum job satisfaction is to you. You should also evaluate your skills, such as writing skills and interpersonal skills. Another important consideration is where you want to live. What climate do you prefer, and would you rather live and work in an urban or a rural community? The answers to these and other questions that you ask yourself will point you in the right direction for finding the kind of job you want.

To conduct a personal assessment you should make a list of factors that are necessary for you to experience satisfaction and contentment in a job. Finance is the first important area to consider:

- Will you have to repay college loans after graduation?
- What are your financial requirements regarding housing, transportation, and family support (if applicable)?
- How much money do you want to make in the future?

Next consider your personal preferences:

- Do your like working alone or interacting with others?
- Do you enjoy working on computers?
- How much supervision do you prefer?
- Do you like assisting others in dealing with and solving their problems?
- How much job-related traveling do you want to do?
- Would you consider job training that required long periods away from your family?
- Are you interested in graduate education to help you advance to a supervisory or executive position?

The third important area to consider is your abilities and deficiencies related to the skills required for your chosen discipline. Among the questions you should ask yourself are the following:

- Are you relaxed when interacting with others?
- Is it easy for you to socialize or converse with people from different social and ethnic-racial backgrounds?
- Are you a self-starter with leadership abilities?
- Are you good at creating ideas and managing projects?
- Are you research oriented and computer literate?
- Are you able to identify and solve problems?
- Are you deadline conscious, or do you procrastinate?
- How well do you work under pressure?

The answers to these and other questions should give you a fairly good perception of your skills and help you match them to the requirements for your desired field.

The fourth important area to consider is job requirements that you may not be able to fulfill that have no bearing on your skills, such as things you cannot or will not do because they conflict with your moral code. For example, if you are considering a job in law enforcement, could you actually shoot someone? Do you believe in capital punishment? If not, could you be involved in sending someone to prison who might be executed?

The fifth important area to consider is the effects of your internship, especially these two questions: Did skills improve during your internship? Did your internship experience verify that the field you wish to enter is the right one for you, or did it convince you to seek a different career path? Use this discussion to assist you in determining the types of jobs that will suit your particular combination of skills and interests, as well as any additional training you wish to pursue.

The final area to consider is geographic location. The necessary questions for this important element are these:

- Do you want to stay in your hometown or state?
- Are you willing to relocate? If so, to what area?
- Do you prefer a warm, cold, or temperate climate?
- Do you prefer urban, suburban, or rural living?
- Can you afford to live in the geographic area that you prefer?

The answers to these questions and others will be helpful in determining whether your career choices are accessible in your desired geographic location.

Two tools are available to assist you in determining the types of employment that may suit you: the *Encyclopedia of Careers and Vocational Guidance* and the

Occupational Outlook Handbook, both of which can be found in the reference section of most libraries. The encyclopedia is in four volumes. Volume 1 describes a wide range of professions. Each entry contains an overview of the profession, including career opportunities, educational requirements, and philosophy. Volumes 2, 3, and 4 present detailed information on several hundred professions, including a brief history, nature of the work, working conditions, requirements, opportunities for education and exploration, techniques for entry and advancement, and information on earnings. The handbook, a smaller version of the encyclopedia, includes information on over 200 careers and affords the same details. Both guides provide information on conventional and mainstream jobs and various unusual ones, but the handbook describes more criminal justice-related occupations such as corrections officers.

Now that you have a fairly good perception of the type of job you want to obtain, you are ready to update or prepare your résumé.

PREPARING THE RÉSUMÉ

Whether you are updating your résumé or preparing one for the first time, you may feel frustrated attempting to compose a one-page marketing tool that will provide a good first impression of you to a complete stranger. Many of my students have shared their frustration with me, and the experience has been even more distressing for those who have not participated in extracurricular activities or held any part-time summer jobs because the purpose of a résumé is to obtain interviews, but until they are interviewed, prospective employers will judge them only by how they present themselves in their résumés. My advice to them, as it is to you, is that there are several types of résumés that will represent you in such a way that employers will want to interview you. You can use the instructions presented here as a guide, but a great deal will depend on your ability to portray your experiences distinctly, concisely, and impressively and produce a high-quality marketing product.

Basic Instructions

1. Usually, human resource personnel take a minute or less to study résumés, so your résumé must be well organized, legible, and well written and must highlight your special qualities. The career center staff at your school can help you write your résumé, and there are commercial services that will write your résumé for a fee. However, I recommend that you prepare your own résumé because you will be more familiar with the information you wish to convey and hence will be more comfortable during an interview. Furthermore, professionally prepared résumés cause interviewers to question their contents and create the impression that you lack the skills required to represent yourself in writing. You should use a résumé service only as a

last resort if you cannot obtain assistance from any other resources mentioned here.

2. Be brief. Use short, clear, and informative sentences. Most employers prefer one-page résumés, which are usually sufficient for college graduates' experiences. It is not unusual to have to prepare several drafts before you are satisfied with the finished product.

3. The educational, work-experience, school, and community-involvement sections will provide the most positive impression of you as a candidate, so begin your résumé with the section that is most impressive and will more likely pique the reader's curiosity about you.

4. *Do not include negative information!* This is not a time to discuss your deficiencies, only your strong points. Remember that you are marketing yourself, and although your résumé should be accurate, it should also be selective. The goal is to make yourself as attractive as possible.

5. Finally, *never* send out a résumé without having it critiqued by someone. The preferable person to show your résumé to is your internship coordinator. However, if for some reason you do not respect his or her writing skills, show it to the career planning or writing center staff at your university, or if all else fails, contact an instructor in the English Department. For the contents of two different types of résumés, see the samples in Figures 3.2 and 3.3.

INVESTIGATING EMPLOYMENT OPPORTUNITIES

Your internship may be the initial introduction to the professional field of your choice. At the beginning of the internship, you should become attentive to professional opportunities that may be available to you later because of this experience. You can learn about career opportunities, entry-level processes, and qualifications for positions at your agency upon graduation by questioning your internship supervisor and co-workers. During your internship, you may also be able to investigate employment opportunities with other agencies and organizations that interact with your agency. For example, while one student was interning at a residential treatment facility for juvenile delinquents, she discovered that the Juvenile Assessment Center was interviewing for caseworkers. She interviewed, was accepted for the position, and is currently working at that center. Several of my students have learned about jobs this way, and others have been hired by their internship agencies. Thus, even if you are unable to obtain a position with your host agency, you have a good opportunity during your internship to network with professional contacts in the criminal justice field that you have made during your internship.

Before you complete your internship, I suggest that you get your supervisors' and co-workers' consent to list them as references on employment applications.

Although it is not illegal to use someone's name as a reference without his or her permission, it is customary to obtain permission. It is also appropriate to request a letter of recommendation from your supervisor, which should include the period of the internship, your responsibilities, your ability to perform those responsibilities, and his or her opinion of your candidacy for a position in the agency's discipline. Because these letters can be extraordinarily significant, you should give considerable thought to requesting them and observe specific fundamental courtesies to make the supervisor's work as simple as possible.

Before you request a letter of recommendation, be sure that you did the best work possible during your internship, as evidenced by the midterm and final evaluations prepared by your agency supervisor and internship coordinator. If you think or your evaluations have determined that your work has not been of the highest quality, you may want to ask your supervisor in person if he or she will write a positive recommendation for you. Even when you think your work deserves a positive recommendation, it is a good idea to mention your specific goals when requesting a letter because, whereas your supervisor may feel awkward supporting some of your vocational aspirations, he or she may be comfortable writing a recommendation for a specific job or graduate program.

Once you have obtained permission to use your supervisors and co-workers as references and acquired letters of recommendation, you will be ready either to prepare or update your résumé, including your internship experience, any other additional part-time employment, and extracurricular activities. If your professional objective has been influenced by your internship experience, this change should be shown in your updated résumé. For example, Michelle, the student mentioned in the sample résumé in Chapter 3, was unhappy with her internship training and wanted more hands-on experience. If Michelle decided to seek part-time summer employment in the same field, she would need to include her desire to be involved in hands-on activities with clients in her professional objectives. She would also add, under relevant courses, "Internship with the Bureau of Prisons, Community Corrections Division," and state the duties she performed.

The cover letter that accompanies the résumé is the final document you need to prepare. The cover letter gives the prospective employer the first impression of you. Make sure that it is a basic, well-prepared letter with no errors. In it, you should introduce yourself as a recent graduate who majored or minored in criminal justice; indicate your area of interest, such as juvenile delinquency or law enforcement; mention your internship education; and state why you are interested in the specific job for which you are applying. If you do not own a personal computer (PC), use one at the school library, and copy the cover letter onto a disk on which you can make changes based on the various positions for which you will apply. See Figure 3.4 for a sample cover letter.

Once your cover letter, résumé, and letters of recommendation are completed, you have received information on employment opportunities from your supervisors and co-workers and obtained guidance from the university's career placement and planning center, your next step is to explore other key sources. These sources may include the Internet, contacts made through networking, classified advertisements in daily newspapers and professional journals, state and federal employment agencies, and the U.S. government.

The newest source of information about employment opportunities is the Internet. If you have a PC and modem, access to the Internet through companies such as Prodigy or America Online and software such as Netscape or Mosaic, that enables you to "surf" the Internet, you can gain access to a wealth of information in this area. If you do not have a PC or access to the Internet, most universities' career planning and placement centers do, and the staff will be happy to assist you in your search. There are several sites on the World Wide Web that provide information about investigating employment, that catalog employment opportunities throughout the country, and that allow you to list your résumé. The two that I am familiar with are CareerMosaic, http://www.careermosaic.com, and Yahoo! Classifieds, http://classifieds.yahoo.com. Some additional websites that can be accessed to learn about career opportunities in the criminal justice are Criminal Justice Net: http://www.criminal-justice.net, Criminology and Criminal Justice: http://www.soc.umn.edu/~overall/crime.htm, Criminology Resources on the Net: http://adhocalypse.arts.unimelb.edu.au/Dept/Crim, The National Institute of Justice: http://www.ojp.usdoj.gov/nij.

Networking with your internship coordinator, other faculty members, classmates, other acquaintances, and relatives can be beneficial in your job search. Your internship coordinator and other members of the criminal justice faculty are excellent resources because their networking relationships in the profession keep them informed of available positions in the field. Make a list of other people you know who work in the field of your choice or who know someone who does, contact these persons, and ask them for tips. Also ask them to circulate your résumé and get their permission to contact them periodically.

Of the resources mentioned, newspapers are the least beneficial because they carry few advertisements for criminal justice positions. However, it is still advisable to get the Sunday edition of the major newspaper in your area that devotes an entire section to classified advertisement. If you are interested in living and working in a particular city, it will be helpful to subscribe to that city's Sunday newspaper as well. Even though the information may be two to three days old by the time you receive the newspaper, it will be an indicator of the types of positions that are available and the deadlines for applying for them. Professional journals in criminal justice and related fields can be found in your university's library.

Advertisements for civil service positions are usually located on bulletin boards in state, country, and federal buildings and employment offices. Most of these positions require written examinations, and the details on the examinations are included in these notices. Information on the geographic locations and salaries of jobs are also provided, so you can compare your career goals with available positions. If you are interested in employment with the U.S. government, your local telephone directory will list the Federal Job Information Center in your area.

Interviewing

Now that your cover letter and résumé have gotten you an interview with an agency in a community that you feel is right for you, the next step is to become as knowledgeable as you can about the agency and the community before the interview. After you get this additional information, your task will be to sell yourself to the agency. During your interview, employers will be interested in your appearance, demeanor, communication skills, educational background, employment experiences, and long-term goals.

Appearance

Your appearance is usually the first criterion by which you are judged during an interview. The interviewer has his or her personal standards of appearance, along with any the agency may require, that you must meet during the interview. It is always safe to wear a traditional, conservative outfit to the interview:

- *Men:*   A dark suit, a white shirt, a striped or softly designed tie, black dress shoes, a dark overcoat, and a touch of cologne, if any. If you live in a warm climate, it is appropriate to eliminate the suit jacket and overcoat.
- *Women:*   A dark suit is still preferred, although off-white, beige, and tan suits are becoming more acceptable in warm climates. A white blouse, solid-color coordinating scarf (if desired), pumps, and hosiery are a must.

Briefcases are recommended because they give the appearance of professionalism. For additional information on dressing for the interviews, see Chapter 3.

Demeanor

The interviewer will learn a great deal about you from your demeanor (body language). Is your facial expression open and friendly, or do you look "mad at the world"? Body language is impressive, and although it is nonverbal, it communicates important information to the interviewer about your confidence and attention span. The following are a few ways to make it work in your favor:

1. Upon meeting your interviewer, make eye contact, smile, and give a strong handshake when introducing yourself. Since we live in a multicultural

society, it is wise to learn the interviewer's background and customs, when possible, so that you do not send the wrong messages with your body language. For example, in some cultures and religions, men do not shake hands with women.

2. Present good posture by walking, standing, and sitting straight. When sitting, do not lean forward or cross your arms in a threatening or hostile position, but sit in an open, unguarded position. Folding your hands in your lap is quite appropriate.

3. Be and look attentive. Do not squirm, tap your fingers, or fiddle with jewelry or your hair.

Communication Skills

Speak with enthusiasm. Without overdoing it, show some excitement about the possibility of working in this aspect of your chosen career. Be aware of the following techniques and role-play the interview with someone to practice your communication skills prior to the interview:

1. Organize your thoughts into logical sentences and verbalize them clearly and grammatically.

2. When answering questions, be precise; offer sufficient information to answer the questions, saying neither too much nor too little. There are times when yes or no answers are necessary, but interviewers usually want you to give more extensive answers. You do not want them to think that by being vague you are trying to be evasive.

3. Most professions use special terms or jargon. For example, "ghosting" is used in one juvenile correctional facility together with the name of a midnight-shift employee (for example, "Terry's ghosting") to indicate that Terry cannot be found and is probably sleeping somewhere. You may have picked up some of these terms during your internship. Before the interview, you may want to visit the library, access the Internet, or contact someone who is working in the field to become familiar with some of these professional terms.

Educational Background

Be prepared for the interviewer to ask the following questions about your educational background:

1. Why did you attend your particular college or university?

2. Of your courses, which did you enjoy and which did you least prefer, and why?

3. What were the most exciting times of your college career, and why?

4. What was your grade-point average? Was it as high as it could have been? If not, why not?

5. What kind of extracurricular activities and community service were you involved in?

6. Did you graduate on time? If not, why not?

Practice answering these questions before the interview and remember to communicate all answers as positively as possible.

Employment Experience

It will be obvious from your résumé whether you have an employment history. If you do, you may encounter such questions as these: What attracted you to your previous jobs, and what were your reasons for leaving? What kind of experience did you gain? What did you enjoy about the work, and what did you dislike? What kind of relationship did you have with your supervisor? What are you looking for in a job? Why are you attracted to this job? In answering these questions, you want to impress on the interviewer that you are ambitious, intelligent, and confident—in short, the best person for the job.

Long-Term Goals

When this questions arises, be prepared to answer it in generalities. At this time in your life, the interviewer will not expect you to have mapped out a ten- or twenty-year plan. For example, you could respond that you are interested in pursuing a wide range of experiences that would assist in your professional development and that would eventually enable you to move into a leadership role in the organization. If these wide-ranging experiences include continuing your education and acquiring a graduate degree, discuss these aspirations in light of their empowering you to make worthwhile contributions to the organization and professional field.

CONTINUING EDUCATION

After graduation, some students choose to acquire a few years of criminal justice-related experience (especially those who have been hired by their internship agencies), while others enroll in law school or graduate programs in various disciplines. You will find that considering your career goals at the beginning of your internship experience comes in handy at this point because knowing your goals is crucial in determining the best graduate program for you. Students who are majoring in criminal justice-criminology may be interested in acquiring graduate degrees in criminal justice, criminology, social work, sociology, psychology, business or public administration, or the law. Once you have decided on the discipline, the next step is to learn which schools and programs fit your needs. If this information is not provided by your department, you may find graduate and law school directories that contain such pertinent information as descriptions of programs, academic requirements, costs, and locations in the university's library or career center.

The career center can also provide you with relevant information on deadlines for applications and required examinations. It is recommended that you make these inquiries at least a semester before you graduate. If you are considering law school, the earlier you inquire about the study programs available to assist you with the Law School Aptitude Test (LSAT), the better, since some students have had to repeat this examination to attain acceptable scores. Again, remember to get advice from your internship coordinator, other faculty members, and prelaw counselor in choosing a suitable discipline and school.

SUMMARY

In this chapter we have discussed issues related to determining the type of position you want, preparing a résumé that will help you obtain a position, locating the position, and preparing for interviews, as well as considerations related to graduate education.

To set your career goals, you have to assess your personal requirements, skills, and the geographic area in which you want to work. This chapter has covered several steps that will help you in evaluating these important areas. You will also find that the *Encyclopedia of Careers and Vocational Guidance* and the *Occupational Outlook Handbook* are two important sources of information on criminal justice and criminology-related occupations. Several factors to consider when updating or preparing a résumé are also discussed here, as are sources of information on job searches, including the Internet, which is the most current resource for locating employment information. Once you have completed the job search and have been offered an interview, follow closely the suggestions prepared here regarding your appearance, demeanor, communication skills, and other important factors discussed here.

Regardless of which path you choose, as you proceed down life's highway, periodically assess your personal aspirations, skills, and geographic choices, which may change over time as you expand your horizons and develop new professional and business relationships.

DISCUSSION QUESTIONS

1. What factors should a person consider when choosing a job?
2. What document needs to be prepared before beginning the job application process? What should this document include?
3. How should one prepare for the job hunting process? Because it is competitive, what guidelines should one follow to make the most lasting impressions?
4. What other educational opportunities are available if one chooses to put off the career option?

References

Applebaum, P. S. "Statutes Regarding Patient–Therapist Sex." *Hospital and Community Psychiatry*, 41 (1990):15–16.

Baird, B., ed. *The Internship, Practicum, and Field Placement Handbook: A Guide for the Helping Professions*. Upper Saddle River, NJ: Prentice Hall, 1996.

Baker, R., and Meyer, F. A., Jr. *The Criminal Justice Game: Politics and Players*. North Scituate, MA: Duxbury Press, 1980.

Bankston, K. "Internship with the Bureau of Prisons." Unpublished manuscript, 1997.

Barnett, B. G. "The Mentor–Intern Relationship: Making the Most of Learning from Experience." *NASSP Bulletin*, 75 (May 1990):17–24.

Bennett, B. E., Bryant, B. K., VandenBos, G. R., and Greenwood, A. *Professional Liability and Risk Management*. Washington, DC: American Psychological Association, 1990.

Bent, A. E., *The Politics of Law Enforcement: Conflict and Power in Urban Communities*. Lexington, MA: D.C. Heath, 1974.

Black, D. "The Legal Ins and Outs of Internship." *Perspective: The Campus Legal Monthly* (December 12, 1987):15–25.

Blackwelder, H. B., and Moorman, W. E. *Internships in Criminal Justice*. Raleigh, NC: Department of Administration, 1975–1976.

Blau, P. M. *Exchange and Power in Social Life*. New York: Wiley, 1964.

Boryrs, D. S., and Pope, K. S. "Dual Relationships between Therapist and Client: A National Study of Psychologists, Psychiatrists and Social Workers." *Professional Psychology: Research and Practice*, 20 (1989):232–242.

California Youth Authority. *CYA Annual Report 2001 Program Description and and Statistical Summary* 1941–2001. Sacramento, CA CYA Resource Library, 2003.

Carlson, N. A. *The Development of the Federal Prison System*. Washington, DC: Unicor, Federal Prison System, 1994.

Cecil, C. "Summer Internship Florida Department of Corrections and Probation." Unpublished manuscript, 1996.

Chambliss, W. J. "Policing the Ghetto Underclass: The Politics of Law and Law Enforcement." *Social Problems*, 41 (1994):177–194.

Chastain, J. "The Summer Internship—What's in It for You." *The Black Collegian*, 92 (January–February 1990):179–180.

Clairborn, C. D., Berberoglu, L. S., Nerison, R. M., and Somberg, D. R. "The Client's Perspective: Ethical Judgments and Perceptions of Therapist's Practice." *Professional Psychology: Research and Practice*, 25 (1994):268–274.

Cole, G. F. "The Decision to Prosecute." *Law and Society Review*, 4 (1970):331–344.

Cox, S. M., and Wade, J. E. *The Criminal Justice Network*, 3rd ed. New York: McGraw-Hill, 1998.

Dudley, J. S. "Learning through Field Experience." In O. Milton and Associates, eds., *On College Teaching*. San Francisco: Jossey-Bass, 1980, pp. 12–16.

Fisher, B., *Techniques of Crime Scene Investigation*, New York: Meridian, 2000.

Florida Department of Corrections. *Annual Report 1995–1996*. 2000–2001 Tallahassee, FL: Bureau of Research and Data Analysis, 2002.

Flowers, R. B., *Minorities and Criminality*. New York: Praeger, 1988.

Gordon, G. R., and McBride, B. *Criminal Justice Internship: Theory into Practice*, 2nd ed. Cincinnati, OH: Anderson, Publishing, 1990.

Greenberg, D. "Intern Hell." *The New Republic* (December 10, 1990):15–16.

Gutheil, T. G., and G. O. Gabbard. "The Concept of Boundaries in Clinical Practice: Theoretical and Risk Management Dimensions." *American Journal of Psychiatry*, 150 (1993):188–196.

Hellebrand, A. "Introspective and Reflective: An Internship at the JRE Lee Opportunity School." Unpublished manuscript, 2003.

Henderson, M. B. "Family. Intervention Specialty Program Internship." Unpublished manuscript, 1995.

Hersh, J. B. and K. Poey. "A Proposed Interviewing Guide for Intern Applicants." In R. H. Dana and W. T. May, eds., *Internship Training in Professional Psychology*. Washington, DC: Hemisphere Publishing Corporation, 1987, pp. 217–220.

Homestead Police Department. *Annual Report*. Homestead, FL: Homestead City Council, 1995.

Howing, P. T., and Wodarski, J. S. "Legal Requisites for Social Workers in Child Abuse and Neglect Situations." *Social Work*, 37 (1992):330–335.

Hoy, W. K. and Miskel, C. G. *Educational Administration: Theory, Research, and Practice*. New York: Random House, 1978.

"Industrial Internships Provide Physics Students with Valuable Experience." *Physics Today* (September 1991):93–94.

Jacksonville Sheriff's Office. *Employment Information Brochure*. Jacksonville, FL: Department of Law Enforcement, 2003.

Jorgenson, L., R. Randel, and L. Strasburger. "The Furor Over Psychotherapist–Patient Sexual Conduct: New Solutions to an Old Problem." *William and Mary Law Review*, 32 (1991):643–729.

Kagle, J. D., and Giebelhausen, P. N. "Dual Relationships and Professional Boundaries." *Social Work*, 39(1994):213–220.

Kazmierczak, M. "Internship: Miami Halfway House." Unpublished manuscript, 2003.

Keyman, F. I. *A Guide for Participation in University Internships in Law Enforcement.* Carbondale, IL: Southern Illinois University Press, December 1997.

Khoury, J. "An Overview of Internships." Unpublished manuscript, 1993.

Kitchener, K. S. "Intuition, Critical Evaluation and Ethical Principles: The Foundation for Ethical Decisions in Psychology." *The Counselor Psychologist*, 12 (1984): 43–56.

Kitchener, K. S. "Dual Relationships: What Makes Them So Problematic?" *Journal of Counseling and Development*, 67 (1988):217–221.

Kleinig, J., and Smith, M. L. *Teaching Criminal Justice Ethics: Strategic Issues.* Cincinnati, OH: Anderson Publishing, 1997.

Kramer, M. "What Can Be Done?" *Time* (May 1, 1992):41–42.

LaFave, W., and Scott, A. W., Jr. *Criminal Law.* St. Paul, MN: West Publishing, 1972.

Lam, T. "Criminology Internship at the Office of the State Attorney." Unpublished manuscript, 2003.

Lasswell, H. *Politics: Who Gets What, When, and How?* New York: Meridian, 1958.

Livingston, J. *Crime and Criminology*, 2nd ed. Upper Saddle River, NJ: Prentice Hall, 1996.

Lofland, J., and Lofland, L. *Analyzing Social Settings: A Guide to Qualitative Observation and Analysis*, 2nd ed. Belmont, CA: Wadsworth, 1984.

Lozada, C., "Miami Halfway House." Unpublished manuscript, 2003.

Mann, C. R. *Unequal Justice: A Question of Color.* Bloomington: Indiana University Press, 1993.

Neely-Scott, T. "Jumpstarting Your career at JRE Lee:," Unpublished manuscript, 2003.

Neubauer, D. W. *American's Courts and the Criminal Justice System*, 4th ed. Pacific Grove, CA: Brooks/Cole, 1992.

Newman, D. "Pleading Guilty for Considerations: A Study of Bargain Justice." *Journal of Criminal Law*, 37 (1970):665.

Norcross, J. C., Strausser, D. J., and Faltus, F. J. "The Therapist's Therapist." *American Journal of Psychotherapy*, 42 (1988):53–66.

Nowell, D., and Spruill, J. "If It's Not Absolutely Confidential, Will Information Be Disclosed?" *Professional Psychology: Research and Practice*, 24 (1993):367–369.

Paradise, L. V., and Kirby, P. C. "Some Perspectives on the Legal Liability of Group Counseling in Private Practice." *Journal of Specialists in Group Work*, 2 (1990):114–118.

Parsons, Talcott. *The Social System.* New York: Free Press, 1951

Permaul, J. "Monitoring and Supporting Experimental Learning." Washington, DC: National Society for Internships and Experimental Education, 1981.

Perrow, C. "The Analysis of Goals in Complex Organizations." *American Sociological Review*, 26 (April 1961): 854–865.

Pitts, J. H. "Organizing a Practicum and Internship Program in Counselor Education." *Counselor Education and Supervision*, 31 (1992):196–207.

Pope, K. S., and Vetter, V. V. "Ethical Dilemmas Encountered by Members of the American Psychological Association: A National Survey." *American Psychologist*, 47 (1992): 397–411.

Rubanowitz, D. E. "Public Attitudes Toward Psychotherapist-Client Confidentiality." Professional Psychology: *Research and Practice*, 18 (1987): 613–618.

Samuelson, B. "Lessons Learned at Troy Academy." Unpublished manuscript, 2003.

Santos, G. "Internship Report—Guardian Ad Litem." Unpublished manuscript, 1997.

Schultz, M. "Internships in Sociology: Liability Issues and Risk Management Measures." *Teaching Sociology*, 20 (July 1992):183–191.

Scott, F. G. "Action Theory and Research in Social Organization." *American Journal of Sociology*, 64 (January 1959):386–395.

Scott, M. E. "Internships Add Value to College Recruitment." *Personnel Journal* (April 1992):59–63.

Stadler, H. and R. D. Paul. "Counselor Educators' Preparation In Ethics." *Journal of Counseling and Development*, 64 (1986): 328–330.

Strasburger, L. H., Jorgenson, L., and Randel, R. "Criminalization of Psychotherapist-Patient Sex." *American Journal of Psychiatry*, 148 (1991):859–863.

Suelzle, M., and Borzak, L. "Stages of Fieldwork." In L. Borzak, ed., *Field Study: A Sourcebook for Experimental Learning*. Thousand Oaks, CA: Sage Publications, 1981.

Swenson, L. C. *Psychology and Law for the Helping Professions*. Pacific Grove, CA: Brooks/Cole, 1993.

Taylor, D. *Jumpstarting Your Career: An Internship Guide for Criminal Justice* Upper Saddle River, Prentice Hall. 1991

Taylor, D. L., and R. L. Bing III. "Racial Discrimination in the Juvenile Justice System: Some Unanswered Questions" *Challenge* 6(2) (December 1995):5–28.

Taylor, D. L., F. Biafora, Jr., and G. Warheit. "Racial Mistrust and Disposition to Deviance Among African American, Haitian, and other Caribbean Island Adolescent Boys." *Law and Human Behavior*, 18 (3) (1994):291–303.

The Criminal Justice Distance Learning Consortium, *The Definitive Guide to Criminal Justice and Criminology on the World Wide Web*. Upper Saddle River, NJ: Prentice Hall, pp. 35–36.

U.S. Department of Justice. "How to Become a DEA Special Agent." *DEA Resources for Job Applicants*. Washington, DC: U. S. Drug Enforcement Administration., 2003a.

U.S. Department of Justice. *Special Agent Employment Brochure*. Washington, DC: U.S. Federal Bureau of Investigation, 2003b.

U.S. Department of Justice. *Bureau of Prisons Goals for 1995 and Beyond*. Lompoc, CA: Federal Bureau of Prisons, 1995.

University of Miami, *Sociology/Criminology Internship Pamphlet*, Department of Sociology, 2003

Vesper, J. H., and Brock, G. W. *Ethics, Legalities, and Professional Practice Issues in Marriage and Family Therapy*. Boston: Allyn and Bacon, 1990.

Walsh, J. A. "From Clinician to Supervisor: Essential Ingredients for Training." *Families in Society*, 71 (2) (1990):82–87.

Walters, L. S. "Anticrime Wave Shackles State Educational Spending." *The Christian Science Monitor* (February 1995):2–11.

Weber, M. *The Theory of Social and Economic Organization*. London: William Hodge, 1947.

Wennes, L. B. "Find Work Now to Dazzle Employers Later." *National Business Employment Weekly* (Spring/Summer 1993):31–32.

Wilson, J. Q., *Varieties of Police Behavior*. Cambridge: Harvard University Press, 1968.

Woodward, B., and Armstrong, S. *The Brethren: Inside the Supreme Court*. New York: Simon and Schuster, 1979.

Zakutansky, T. J. and E. A. Sirles. "Ethical and Legal Issues in Field Education: Shared Responsibility and Risk. *Journal of Social Work Education*, 29 (1993):338–347.

Index

Resource Guide

This guide provides various criminal justice agencies, listed alphabetically by states, that will assist you in entering the world of work in 25 major cities in the United States taken from the *Statistical Abstract of the United States 2000: The National Data Book*. The agencies represented here are Federal Bureau of Investigation (FBI), juvenile justice agencies, probation and parole offices, police departments, and the Secret Service. This listing represents only a small number of criminal justice agencies but does provide a valuable starting point.

1. Phoenix, AZ

   FBI
   201 East Indianaola Avenue,
      Suite 400
   Phoenix, AZ 85012
   (602) 279-5511

   Department of Juvenile Justice
   1624 West Adams Street
   Phoenix, AZ 85007
   (602) 542-3987

   Department of Probation
   1022 East Garfield Street
   Phoenix, AZ 85006-3236
   (602) 254-7030

   Office of Parole
   6725 35th Street
   Phoenix, AZ 85017
   (602) 255-4147

   Police Department
   135 N-2nd Ave
   Phoenix, AZ 85003-3100
   (602) 495-5009

   U.S. Secret Service
   3200 North Central Avenue,
      Suite 1450
   Phoenix, AZ 85012
   (602) 640-5580

2. Los Angeles, CA

   FBI
   11000 Wilshire Boulevard
   Los Angeles, CA 90024-3602
   (310) 477-6565

   Juvenile Detention
   1605 East Lake Avenue
   Los Angeles, CA 90033-1009
   (213) 226-8616

Probation Office
312 North Spring Street
Los Angeles, CA 90012
1-213-894-3600

Department of Parole
600 St. Paul Ave.
Los Angeles, CA 90017
1-213-977-6868

Police Department
110 East Ninth Street
Los Angeles, CA 90079
(213) 624-6042

U.S. Secret Service
255 East Temple Street
Los Angeles, CA 90012
(213) 894-4830

3. San Diego, CA

FBI
915 Second Avenue, Suite 710
San Diego, CA 92101-8897
(619) 231-1122

Juvenile Justice Department
324 Apple Still Road
San Diego, CA 92101
(619) 531-2495

Department of Probation
4004 Kearny Mesa Road
San Diego, CA 92110-3730
(619) 560-1837

Department of Parole
4004 Kearny Mesa Road
San Diego, CA 92110-3730
(619) 560-1850

Police Department
1401 Broadway
San Diego, CA 92101
(619) 521-2777

U.S. Secret Service
550 West C Street, Suite 660
San Diego, CA 92101
(619) 557-5640

4. San Jose, CA

FBI
950 South Bacon St. Ste 300
San Jose, CA 95128-3002
415-553-7400

Juvenile Hall
840 Guadalupe Parkway
San Jose, CA 95110-1714
(408) 299-3481

Office of Probation
280 South First Street
San Jose, CA 95113-3002
(408) 291-7671

Office of Parole
165 Lewis Road
San Jose, CA 95111-2158
510-622-4701

Police Department
55 West Younger Avenue
San Jose, CA 95110
(408) 211-2220

U.S. Secret Service
280 South First Street,
   Suite 1111
San Jose, CA 95113
888-813-8777

5. San Francisco, CA

FBI
345 Spear St. Suite 530
San Francisco, CA 94105
(415) 744-9026

Juvenile Office of San Mateo
455 County Center
Redwood City, CA 94063
(650) 312-8816

Department of Probation
850 Bryant Street
San Francisco, CA 94103-4603
(415) 553-1704

Department of Parole
850 Bryant Street
San Francisco, CA 94103-4603
(415) 553-1689

Police Department
766 Vallejo Street
San Francisco, CA 94133-3818
(415) 315-2400

U.S. Secret Service
345 Spear Street,
   Suite 530
San Francisco, CA 94105
(415) 744-9020

6. Denver, CO

FBI
1961 Stout Street,
   Suite 1823
Denver, CO 80294
(303) 629-7171

Juvenile Corrections
4255 South Knox Court
Denver, CO 80236
(303) 866-7345

Department of Probation
303 West Colfax Avenue
Denver, CO 80204
(303) 640-2971

Office of Parole
116 Inverness Drive East
Englewood, CO 80112
(303) 784-6126

Police Department
4685 Peoria Street
Denver, CO 80239
(303) 576-2897

U.S. Secret Service
1660 Lincoln Street
Denver, CO 80264-3101
(303) 866-1010

7. Washington, DC

FBI
1900 Half Street SW
Washington, DC 20024
(202) 252-7801

Youth Center Corrections
   Department
1923 Vermont Avenue, NW
Washington, DC 20001-4103
(202) 643-2234

Office of Probation
401 New York Avenue NE
Washington, DC 20001-4628
(202) 675-9183

Office of Parole
717 14th Street NW
Washington, DC 20005-3203
(202) 727-2264

Police Department
320 First Street NW
Washington, DC 20001
(202) 727-9334

U.S. Secret Service
1050 Connecticut Ave NW
Washington, DC 20036-5303
(202) 435-5100

8. Jacksonville, FL

FBI
7820 Arlington Expressway
Jacksonville, FL 32211-7481
(904) 721-1211

Juvenile Detention Center
1241 East Eighth Street
Jacksonville, FL 32206
(904) 798-4834

Department of Probation
4250 Lake Side Drive
Jacksonville, FL 32210
(904) 381-6000

Department of Parole
4250 Lake Side Drive
Jacksonville, FL 32210
(904) 381-6100

Police Department
501 East Bay Street
Jacksonville, FL 32203
(904) 630-7600

U.S. Secret Service
7820 Arlington Expressway
Jacksonville, FL 32211-7481
(904) 724-4530

9. Chicago, IL

FBI
219 South Dearborn Street,
   Suite 905
Chicago, IL 60604-1705
(312) 431-1333

Juvenile Tempy Detention Center
1100 South Hamilton Avenue
Chicago, IL 60612-4207
(312) 738-8200

Department of Probation
2600 South California Avenue
Chicago, IL 60608
(773) 869-3280

Department of Parole
2600 South California Avenue
Chicago, IL 60608
(773) 869-3300

Police Department
2259 South Damen Avenue
Chicago, IL 60606-6613
(312) 353-2212

U.S. Secret Service
525 West Van Buren Ste 900
Chicago, IL 60606-6613
(312) 353-5431

10. Indianapolis, IN

FBI
575 North Pennsylvania Street,
   Suite 679
Indianapolis, IN 46204-1524
(317) 639-3301

Juvenile Corrections Facility
2596 Girl's School Road
Indianapolis, IN 46214-2105
(317) 244-3887

Office of Probation
200 East Washington Street,
   Suite 641
Indianapolis, IN 46204
(317) 327-4252

Indianapolis Parole Office
3921 North Meridian Street
Indianapolis, IN 46208-4011
(317) 931-4375

Police Department
209 East Street Joseph Street
Indianapolis, IN 46204
(317) 327-6500

U.S. Secret Service
575 North Pennsylvania Street,
   Suite 211
Indianapolis, IN 46204-1524
(317) 226-6444

11. Baltimore, MD

FBI
7142 Ambassador Road
Baltimore, MD 21244-2754
(410) 265-8080

Department of Juvenile
   Services
3939 Reisterstown Road
Baltimore, MD 21215-7601
(410) 333-6041

Probation Field Office
217 East Fayette Street
Baltimore, MD 21202-3410
(410) 798-4834

Parole Field Office
217 East Fayette Street
Baltimore, MD 21202-3410
(410) 798-3400

Police Department
601 East Fayette Street
Baltimore, MD 21202
(410) 396-2525

U.S. Secret Service
100 South Charles Street
Baltimore, MD 21201-2725
(410) 962-2200

12. Boston, MA

FBI
One Center Plaza, Suite 600
Boston, MA 02108
(617) 742-5533

Juvenile Center
450 Canterbury Street
Boston, MA 02131-3216
(617) 727-2264

Office of Probation
507 New Court House
Temperton Square
Boston, MA 02108
(617) 725-8426

Office of Parole
27043 Wormwood Street
Boston, MA 02210
(617) 727-3272

Police Department
City Hall
Boston, MA 02201
(906) 482-3100

U.S. Secret Service
10 Causeway Street
Boston, MA 02108
(617) 565-5640

13. Detroit, MI

FBI
477 Michigan Avenue,
26th Floor
Detroit, MI 48226
(313) 965-2323

Juvenile Detention Center
1333 East Forest
Detroit, MI 48207
(313) 833-2905

Department of Probation
426 Clinton Street
Detroit, MI 48226
(313) 224-5000

Office of Parole
1200 Sixth Street
Detroit, MI 48226
(313) 256-2566

Police Department
1300 Beaubien Street
Detroit, MI 48226
(313) 596-2200

U.S. Secret Service
477 Michigan Avenue,
10th Floor
Detroit, MI 48226-2719
(313) 226-6400

14. New York, NY

FBI
26 Federal Plaza, 23rd Floor
New York, NY 10007
(212) 384-1000

Department of Juvenile Justice
365 Broadway
New York, NY 10007
(212) 925-7779

Department of Probation
115 Leonard Street
New York, NY 10013
(212) 442-4293

Department of Parole
3114 West 40th Street
New York, NY 10018
(212) 239-6000

Police Department
41 Main Street
New York, NY 10044-0052
(518) 762-3143

U.S. Secret Service
140 Grand
White Plains, NY 10601
914-682-6300

15. Columbus, OH

FBI
500 South Front Street,
    Suite 1050
Columbus, OH 43215
(614) 224-1183

Juvenile Detention Facility
399 South Front Street
Columbus, OH 43215-4591
(614) 462-4490

Department of Probation Services
373 South High Street
Columbus, OH 43215-4591
(614) 462-3700

Office of Parole
1050 Freeway Drive North
Columbus, OH 43229
(614) 752-1253

Police Department
1611 Chillicothe Street
Columbus, OH 43207
(614) 491-3211

U.S. Secret Service
300 Hancock Street
Columbus, OH 43215
(419) 625-6052

16. Pittsburgh, PA

FBI
700 Grant Street, Suite 300
Pittsburgh, PA 15219-1906
(412) 471-2000